SR. Mary Vincenza, S.S.N.D. entered the School Sisters of Notre Dame in 1959. Since then she has taught in New Jersey, Brooklyn and Rochester, N.Y. She received her B.S. degree in Elementary Education with a concentration in Theology from Seton Hall University, South Orange, N.J., and is pursuing graduate studies in Religious Education at St. John's University, New York.

Sr. Vincenza has wide experience as a consultant in the religious education field and she has also given lectures and conducted workshops, days of recollection, and retreats. She is presently the co-ordinator of religious education for St. Ann's parish in Hornell, New York.

Creative Religion Involvement Programs

Creative
Religion
Involvement
Programs

SR. M. VINCENZA, SSND

ALBA · HOUSE   NEW · YORK

SOCIETY OF ST. PAUL, 2187 VICTORY BLVD., STATEN ISLAND, NEW YORK 10314

Library of Congress Cataloging in Publication Data

Mary Vincenza, Sister, S. S. N. D.
    Creative religion involvement programs.
    Bibliography: p.
    1.   Religious education of young people.
I.   Title.
BV1485.M28   268'.6   73-10212
ISBN 0-8189-0277-9

Nihil Obstat:

Edward Higgins, O.F.M. Cap., S.T.L.
Censor Librorum

Imprimatur:

+James P. Mahoney, D.D.
Vicar General, Archdiocese of New York
May 30, 1973

*Designed, printed and bound in the United States of America by the Fathers
and Brothers of the Society of St. Paul, 2187 Victory Boulevard,
Staten Island, New York 10314, as part of their
communications apostolate.*

9 8 7 6 5 4 3 2   (Current Printing: first digit).

Dedicated to the priests, sisters, teachers, children and parents of Holy Ghost Parish in Rochester, N.Y., who inspired me to write this book and helped make it possible by their hearty cooperation in my projects.

Preface

We have witnessed more spectacular and rapid change in society all over the world during the past decade than in any period in our global history. There is an increasing demand for direct action, for deep involvement, less willingness to accept tradition blindly.

Change is difficult to accommodate; it shakes people up, it shocks them, some into a desire to quickly revolutionize our mores and institutions; and unfortunately, many into apathy.

But change can be healthy and affirmatively productive, when people—parents, teachers, and children are interested enough to be part of what is going on, to probe for greater understanding of social trends and issues, to develop ability to objectively evaluate alternatives, and to press for accountability. The great difference apparent is between involvement of a positive nature and detachment.

The organized profession of public education is showing great concern for improvements in learning and feels the urgency for creating new instructional programs which will help students of all ages to comprehend, face up to, live with, and direct social change. Churches and Church schools are scrutinizing themselves and showing the same depths of concern. Children are questioning the authority of parents and educators. Blind allegiance to Church, school, and family is washing out.

It is my hope that this book, directed toward behavior modification, will reach and help all those who feel concern about the religious education of young people, and will have an abiding impact upon the training of our future generation. It has been written by a master teacher and her students.

Each chapter provides guidelines for the stimulation of active dialogue between learners and teachers; designs are suggested for total involvement of both. In essence, this highly creative program provides a bridge between the frontiers of the humanities and significant discoveries being made about intergroup relations, people, valuing, and learning. It is sensitive to the needs of the young in our changing society for creative ways to face an uncertain future and for an effective set of values upon which to base their actions and their judgments.

Dr. Helen B. Warrin
Associate Professor of Education
Seton Hall University,
South Orange, New Jersey

Acknowledgments

I wish to thank all of those who have contributed to the successful production of this book, especially Dr. Helen B. Warrin of the Elementary Education Department of Seton Hall University who encouraged me to pursue this book and the members of the Faculty and Administration who were instrumental in the writing of it; my Provincial, Sister Mary Petonilla Killigrew, Councilor, Sister Patricia Marie Griffin and the many members of my Community who have encouraged and supported me throughout the years as a Notre Dame sister.

I am also deeply indebted to Mrs. Patricia Dowd and Mrs. Dorothy Rhinebodt of St. Leo's School in Irvington, N.J. who helped me with many of the projects in the book, and to Sister Mary Claude Burns and Sister Marion Amhrein who spent many hours proofreading my work and Sister Michelle Marie Michaels and the mothers of St. Leo's Parish, Irvington, N.J., for their typing services and to Sister Grace Avila, C.S.J. for her cooperation.

Finally, and most gratefully, I wish to acknowledge those who have been closest to me in spirit throughout this project: my beloved deceased parents and my relatives and friends.

Sr. Mary Vincenza, S.S.N.D.

TABLE OF CONTENTS

Creative Religion Involvement Programs

INTRODUCTION TO METHODOLOGY

ONE OF THE MOST important challenges facing teachers of religion today is to actively involve their students in the learning process in such a way that they will be able to relate the Christian doctrine and religious values they learn in class to their everyday lives as committed witnesses to Christ. This is no easy task but difficulty is never a valid excuse for not trying. Educators should be challenged by the following words of St. Paul: "The spirit that has been given to you must not shrink from danger." Many of us educators have failed in our responsibility of bringing Christ to our students and helping them develop themselves into mature Christians. If we truly believe with St. Paul that God is reconciling all things in the world to himself through Christ, then we have to honestly examine the reasons why we so often fail to live the Gospel and imitate Christ in our own lives, thereby failing to communicate the good news of Christ in a convincing manner to our students.

The main thrust of this book is to present involvement programs for students which hopefully will minimize routine and boredom in the classroom and maximize creative expression and a more profound and lasting grasp of the content presented. The really *effective* teacher must be a *creative* teacher who can both plan dynamic programs and be able to draw out the latent talents of the students to make the programs work. Planned and directed student involvement is the key to success.

The PROGRAMS are built around monthly themes which cover the major doctrines of our religion: 1) September: *Crea-*

tion, 2) October: *Pentecost,* 3) November: *Advent,* 4) December: *Incarnation,* 5) January: *Eucharist,* 6) February: *Redemption,* 7) March: *Lent and Penance,* 8) April: *Easter and the Resurrection,* 9) May: *Marian Devotion,* 10) June: *Christ's Second Coming.*

In addition, five SPECIAL PROGRAMS are included: 1) *Book Studies,* 2) *Record Studies,* 3) *Creative Writing Projects,* 4) *People's Day,* 5) *Psychedelic Encounters I* and *II.*

Each of the monthly PROGRAMS is developed in four or five different approaches utilizing audio-visual materials, liturgical and para-liturgical celebrations, group discussions, social and apostolic activities, and other methods of creative expression. The various approaches are all geared to present the widest possible variety of activities and to insure maximum student involvement. While these PROGRAMS are primarily designed for grades 7 to 9, they may also be adapted for use in other grade levels in grammar and high school.

Before presenting the various monthly and special occasion PROGRAMS, it probably will be helpful to teachers, especially beginners, to discuss several of the approaches and techniques which are employed in the various PROGRAMS. They include the preparation and carrying out of liturgical and para-liturgical celebrations, the role of audio-visual aids, creative expression projects, and social and apostolic activities.

Liturgical and Para-liturgical Celebrations

One of the primary and most urgent tasks incumbent upon the creative religion teacher is providing her students with as many opportunities for participation in liturgical and para-liturgical celebrations in the home, school and church building as is feasible.

Although worship and the celebration of life should go together, they are not the same thing. Christian liturgy is not only a celebration of life—it is a celebration of life-transformed-by-faith. The difference should be taught to the students in a meaningful way. They should be made to understand that the urge to celebrate life is universal among men of all times and cultures. The insightful teacher will take advantage of young people's natural, spontaneous urge to communicate to others, in some external manner, the joy they experience interiorly when they have discovered some new insight into life. She must likewise encourage them to express and celebrate and communicate their newly discovered religious values which also affirm life. One of the best ways to make these religious values an integral part of their lives is through a liturgical or para-liturgical celebration. Young people today want to know why they must worship. One way to make their worship of God more intelligible is to show the correlation between the happenings, events and celebrations of their daily lives with their worship of God. In fact, one of the most important fruits of the liturgical renewal given impetus by Vatican II has been the emphasis put upon the liturgy, on the meaning of celebration, and on the deeper experiences of life, love, joy and hope.

The key to an exciting and successful liturgical celebration is getting the students themselves actively involved in preparing the liturgy. In this way the liturgy becomes a part of their personal expression and the Mass becomes a more vital part of their Christian living. The students should be taught to *live* the Mass through their dynamic and creative participation.

Depending on the actual classroom situation, the teacher could either select a liturgical planning committee to prepare the various parts of the Mass, or the class could split into groups to prepare separate parts of the Mass. The teacher could then act as a coordinator.

Recognizing that it is utterly impossible to have a good liturgy unless it is well-planned, the teacher should keep the following suggestions in mind when the class is preparing a liturgy.

1) It is important to have a crisp, clear and easily grasped theme stated before the Mass begins. If the Mass is celebrated on a special day such as Teacher Recognition Day, Graduation Day, Confirmation Day or some special feast day, the students could make banners or posters depicting the special theme of the Mass. These help to create a celebrative atmosphere and are a means of getting the students actively involved.

2) The students could prepare an introduction to each of the Scripture readings, an opening and concluding prayer to the Prayer of the Faithful or they could spontaneously offer their own intentions during the Mass.

3) For each Mass different lectors, readers and servers should be selected. The students themselves could bring up the wine and water and ciborium to the altar at the Offertory. They might also place their own hosts in the ciborium before the Offertory procession, perhaps making a special intention while doing so.

4) The students should also choose the songs for the Mass. Since singing is one of the most important elements of a good liturgical celebration, the songs should be practiced beforehand.

5) It might be beneficial once in a while to supplement the homily with films, filmstrips, slides, tape excerpts, songs from records, or other audio-visual aids.

6) After Communion there could be a meditation period. A record could be played in the background while the students pray and reflect, e.g., "My Sweet Lord" (*The Beatles*), "Bridge Over Troubled Water" (*Simon and Garfunkel*), "The Impossible Dream" (*Robert Goulet*). Or appropriate psalms, religious poems or readings could be read. Or a period of silence may help to foster an atmosphere of reflection and spiritual unity.

7) Other supplemental actions which would enhance the liturgical celebration would be: begin and end the Mass with a procession; have the students gather around the altar for Mass

and join hands during the Our Father and extend the Greeting of Peace to each other and the members of the congregation to express their unity as a class and a worshipping community.

8) If possible, try to arrange a home Mass some evening in one of the student's homes. This often turns out to be a beautiful and inspiring experience for the students and their parents.

The Role of Audio-Visual Aids

Students today are audio-visually oriented—they are constantly exposed to radio, television, tapes, films and filmstrips.

Today there are available to educators many audio-visual aids which are valuable tools for bringing dynamic learning programs into the classroom. They include overhead and opaque projectors, films, filmstrips, records, tapes and cassettes, banners and posters, tape recorders and small, portable movie cameras. They are not meant to, and never can, replace the teacher who alone can work with the students on a person-to-person basis of directing and evaluating. Rather they are intended to facilitate and enhance the learning process by appealing to the senses and involving the *whole* person, not just the intellect, in the learning process. Each teacher will have to determine the utility of any particular audio-visual aid as a supplementary means of instruction in her specific classroom situation.

She should critically preview and carefully select audio-visual materials in view of the interests, needs and backgrounds of her students. And although it will take a great deal of time and energy to correlate the use of audio-visuals with the teacher's overall lesson plans, the creative effort expended will bear much fruit in making the teaching of religion a more productive as well as a more satisfying experience for both students and teachers.

1) An *overhead projector* has multiple uses, e.g., to project a map or teacher's notes on the board to illustrate a lecture or to project a visual stimulus to initiate discussion. Depending on the

teacher's individual style, overhead and even opaque projectors can be creatively utilized to produce exciting and interesting educational programs.

2) Films have a tremendous educational impact upon young people. Films have a unique power to mold young people's ways of thinking and acting, as well as affecting their sense of values. They also touch the person's emotions and elicit patterns of behavior. Therefore, *movie-study programs* which include the viewing of films and follow-up discussions will help students develop a sense of values and a religious outlook on life. Such programs should be aimed at communicating ideas and forming habits of greater awareness, wonder and awe as well as intelligent evaluation, analysis, selectivity, judgment and decision. The teaching of religion can be made more meaningful through film presentations since many films deal honestly and graphically with human values and problems of life. In one of my classes we studied the movie "The Cross and the Switchblade" which deals with the problems of drug abuse. I previewed the movie and then formulated some evaluation questions. After the students viewed the movie, they broke up into groups to discuss the film according to the different categories I had presented. They were assigned: a) character study, b) plot, c) value of one's faith, d) peer group dominance. This was then followed by a general discussion in which they analyzed the movie's content according to Christian principles. Such an approach enables them to intelligently criticize films and sharpen their critical awareness, moral judgments, and emotional sensitivity. During the discussion period the teacher should be prepared to offer guidance and plan the direction that the film critique should take. Such an intelligent study of films can lead to changes in attitudes, in the acceptance of moral obligations, and the establishment of a sense of responsibility, and will make the teaching and learning of religion more meaningful.

3) In the past few years the *filmstrip* approach to religion

teaching has gained in popularity. While the filmstrip offers somewhat less of a visual appeal than the film, there is still a great deal of stimulating imagery which can spark creative thought and evoke effective class discussion concerning the students' attitudes as Christians towards contemporary social concerns, the value of human life, and other crucial issues. Also, filmstrips are much less expensive than films.

4) *Record studies* are also valuable in teaching religious and moral values. Many of the records students listen to today contain messages of a religious or spiritual nature and can be used to initiate interesting and fruitful discussions. For example, the song "Sounds of Silence" (*Simon and Garfunkel*) dramatizes the loneliness of many people who cannot communicate with their fellowmen. "People" (*Barbra Streisand*) stresses the fact that the barriers to communication can be broken when people recognize their need for each other. "Born Free" (*Roger Williams*) explores the question: are we really free when we can't communicate this freedom? The Beatles' song "Getting Better" shows how a little love will help break the barriers of silence.

I realize that the records I have listed here and those which I discuss later in the book were very popular in the late 60's and early 70's and may seem dated to many teachers and students today. In one sense they are since in the pop field the popularity of records is very short-lived. Furthermore, the Beatles are no longer a group and Simon and Garfunkel no longer sing together. However, the songs they and others wrote and recorded can still be regarded as minor classics of an era which gave birth to a striking combination of good music and meaningful lyrics. Their songs poignantly reflect the problems, joys, hopes, and aspirations of young people of all generations and still have a great deal of meaning today. It was with this in mind that I included them as examples. Of course, it will be up to each teacher to decide whether to supplement these songs with more current popular records.

Records can also be used in teaching songs or hymns for the liturgy. The use of records as background music is also effective in creating a reflective mood or atmosphere and may therefore enhance the learning potential of the students.

5) *Audio tapes and cassettes* are also gaining an increasing role in Christian education today. There are many fine audio programs by recognized specialists in the areas of scripture, dogma, moral, liturgy, and other theological disciplines. Not only are they ideal for initiating discussions and exchanges of ideas among students, but they also are an excellent means for teachers to continue furthering their own education. The students should be encouraged to make tapes of some of their own programs and involvement activities. These could then be shared with other classes. Such a procedure is beneficial for teaching students how to organize their material for taping and how to present it in an intelligent and articulate manner.

Creative Expression Projects

For too long creative expression has been thought of as an activity solely for the artistically inclined and talented, to be learned by the less talented only as a means of emotional release. We now know that creative expression is also a means of consolidating, summarizing and reinforcing what a person has learned.

Therefore, art projects, creative writing projects, and dramatizations can be utilized to great advantage in religious education. It is up to the teacher to present the students with these creative tools. Creative activities, in addition to teaching self-discipline, play a part in developing democratic citizenship. Through the arts the student learns respect for individuality. At the same time he learns how to cooperate with his peers, how his role in a dramatization must fit in with that of others, or how his contribution to his group's mural or banner must harmonize with the contributions of others.

There are several *art projects* which could be used to encourage the students to creatively express what they have learned in class. Students are especially interested in making their own banners, posters and other bulletin board displays with special themes. For example, after the class has studied the stories of some of the Old Testament figures, they could draw a picture or make a banner of Moses and the Burning Bush, or make a diorama depicting the scene. Murals, mobiles and collages are also means by which students working in groups can depict incidents they have learned in class. The important point is to encourage the students themselves to draw, paint or cut out the necessary materials. In this way the displays will function as activity projects as well as visual aids.

Creative writing projects are also a valuable means by which the students can express themselves and most of all reveal their personalities to others, thereby helping the insightful teacher to come to a better knowledge of her class. It is amazing to see the ideas that the students will come up with about life, love, freedom and other subjects.

The use of *dramatic presentations* is another method of engaging the creative talents of the students. My class once put on a program of commercials to depict the idea that materialism is slowly leading people away from God. For example, they acted out several of the toothpaste, mouthwash, and make-up commercials. The creative teacher can come up with several other ways to use drama as a medium of learning.

During all of these activities it is a good idea for all the students to have their own notebooks so that they will be able to conveniently organize their notes, pictures and reports.

Social Apostolic Activities

Another effective way to engage the students' attention in religion classes is to encourage them to get involved within their social environment. This enables them to see and live the connection between the religious values they learn in class and their vocations as Christians to help the poor, the sick, and the ignorant to lead more human lives. My class, for example, once invited some culturally-deprived children from a poor area of the city to spend the day at our school. We called it "People's Day" —a "getting-to-know-one-another" time when the students played hosts to their less fortunate neighbors. A chairman and co-chairman were appointed to set up various committees to take care of invitations, refreshments, games, clean-up, and other necessary chores. This active involvement gave the students a sense of accomplishment and importance. They themselves made the day a success by working together as a group.

The innovative teacher will be able to develop similar projects or field trips which will foster the students' social awareness and desire to get involved in some way to make the world a better place in which to live.

Concluding Remarks

Having discussed some of the ideas behind the various programs and having suggested various approaches to effectively implement them, we will now present the programs themselves. It should be noted that directives have been limited to those which are necessary in order to allow teachers the flexibility to adapt the activities to their specific curriculum plans and their own particular style and methods. Also, since there are at least four different approaches to each monthly theme, each teacher can decide, depending on the amount of time available, whether to use one approach each week during the month, or use one approach once a month.

At the end of the book is a resource materials section which includes a selected reading list of books which the teacher may find helpful for background reading and reference work, some of the major periodicals in which religion teachers may find creative insights and ideas, and a list of some of the major sources of audio-visual materials. Since there are new materials constantly being produced, teachers will find it helpful to ask to be placed on these companies' mailing lists so that they can receive the latest catalogues and brochures and be informed of available resource materials which they can effectively use in their religion classes.

For all of the biblical quotations I have used *The Oxford Annotated Bible with the Apocrypha, Revised Standard Version.* Each teacher can freely substitute any other version she prefers.

Creation

FIRST APPROACH:

A discussion based on the filmstrip *Understanding Genesis* (Thomas S. Klise Co., P.O. Box 3418, Peoria, Ill. 61414). In this filmstrip the book of Genesis is used as one of the best examples of the historical process by which the Old Testament as a whole came into being. Picture stories and cartoons are used to illustrate religious truths and values.

OBJECTIVES:

1. To introduce the students to an historical view of the creation story.
2. To make them aware of the figurative language used by the author of Genesis.
3. To foster the students' awareness that they are part of God's creative act.

MATERIALS:

Filmstrip and records, filmstrip projector, screen, notebooks and pencils.

PROCEDURE:

Read the Old Testament story of the creation to the students or assign several students to read it. Then before presenting the filmstrip to them, stress the idea of the figurative language used in the Old Testament. The early Israelites were largely uneducated and happenings and events had to be explained through figurative speech and symbols.

Ask the students what points of the creation story have a special meaning for them. Would they want the creation story explained to them differently or are they satisfied with it as it is written in the Bible?

Show the filmstrip. After the presentation divide the class into small groups and have them discuss the filmstrip. It would be good to give them a few questions as discussion starters. Then a general discussion should follow, at which time a representative from each group will present to the entire class a summary of that group's discussion.

To end the assignment each group should rewrite the creation story in modern terms and then present it to the entire class.

SECOND APPROACH:

The use of two prayer services entitled, "The Creation Story" and its sequel, "Earth's Beginning and Future." This approach combines a learning situation with a prayer experience.

OBJECTIVES:

1.   To have the students recognize the power of God in the creation of the world and to make them realize that they too are co-creators in a certain limited sense.

2.   To foster the students' awareness of each other by having them work together in groups and enter into some kind of meaningful relationship with their peer group.

3.   To combine a learning situation with a prayer service so that the students will realize that prayer is an essential part of their everyday living.

MATERIALS:

A Bible, two candles, a small table or desk, four-color wheels, records for background music, e.g., "Turn, Turn, Turn" (*The Byrds*), "Theme Song from Romeo and Juliet" (*Henry Mancini*), a record player, a string of multi-colored lights.

PROCEDURE:

Explain to the students that they will be studying in some depth the creation story which is found in Genesis 12, 3. The class should break up into six groups with one person assigned as chairman. Also appoint two students to serve as your leader and co-leader.

Assign one of the days of creation to each group and instruct them to refer to the Bible for the verses for which they will be responsible. Each group should have a lector who will read the verses during the services.

During the services the four-color wheels and the string of multi-colored lights should be placed around the semi-darkened room to help set a prayerful atmosphere. A record such as the "Theme Song from Romeo and Juliet" could be played very softly throughout the whole service as background music.

During the first prayer service, "The Creation Story," the students should just relate what happened during the six days of creation. They could illustrate what happened on each day by means of collages, posters, dramatizations, reports or other projects.

During the second prayer service, "Earth's Beginning and Future," they should discuss how they think the earth will be two hundred years from now.

During the discussion period you and your two leaders should walk around and sit in on various group discussions and serve as resource persons and guides.

2

The following are suggested outlines for the two prayer services:

I. THE CREATION STORY[1]

Leader:
"In the beginning God created the heavens and the earth. The earth was without form and void, and darkness was upon the face of the deep; and the Spirit of God was moving over the face of the waters" (Gen 1, 1-2).

HYMN: "All the Earth Proclaim the Lord"

THE FIRST DAY:
And God said, "Let there be light"; and there was light. And God saw that the light was good; and God separated the light from the darkness. God called the light Day, and the darkness he called Night. And there was evening and there was morning, one day (Gen 1, 3-5).

CHAIRMAN I: Display and explain poster.

THE SECOND DAY:
And God said, "Let there be a firmament in the midst of the waters, and let it separate the waters from the waters." And God made the firmament and separated the waters which were under the firmament from the waters which were above the firmament. And it was so. And God called the firmament Heaven. And there was evening and there was morning, a second day (Gen 1, 6-8).

---

1. All Scripture quotations are from the Revised Standard Version Bible and used by permission.

CHAIRMAN II: *Display and explain collage.*

THE THIRD DAY:
And God said, "Let the waters under the heavens be gathered together into one place, and let the dry land appear." And it was so. God called the dry land Earth, and the waters that were gathered together he called Seas. And God saw that it was good. And God said, "Let the earth put forth vegetation, plants yielding seed, and fruit trees bearing fruit in which is their seed, each according to its kind, upon the earth." And it was so. The earth brought forth vegetation, plants yielding seed according to their own kinds, and trees bearing fruit in which is their seed, each according to its kind. And God saw that it was good. And there was evening and there was morning, a third day (Gen 1, 9-13).

CHAIRMAN III: *Display and explain banner.*

THE FOURTH DAY:
And God said, "Let there be lights in the firmament of the heavens to separate the day from the night; and let them be for signs and for seasons and for days and years, and let them be lights in the firmament of the heavens to give light upon the earth." And it was so. And God made the two great lights, the greater light to rule the days, and the lesser light to rule the night; he made the stars also. And God set them in the firmament of the heavens to give light upon the earth, to rule over the day and over the night, and to separate the light from the darkness. And God saw that it was good. And there was evening and there was morning, a fourth day (Gen 1, 14-19).

CHAIRMAN IV: *Display and explain poster.*

THE FIFTH DAY:
And God said, "Let the waters bring forth swarms of living

creatures, and let birds fly above the earth across the firmament of the heavens." So God created the great sea monsters and every living creature that moves, with which the waters swarm, according to their kinds, and every winged bird according to its kind. And God saw that it was good. And God blessed them, saying, "Be fruitful and multiply and fill the waters in the seas, and let birds multiply on the earth." And there was evening and there was morning, a fifth day (Gen 1, 20-23).

CHAIRMAN V: *Display and explain poster.*

THE SIXTH DAY:
And God said, "Let the earth bring forth living creatures according to their kinds: cattle and creeping things and beasts of the earth according to their kinds." And it was so. And God made the beasts of the earth according to their kinds and the cattle according to their kinds, and everything that creeps upon the ground according to its kind. And God saw that it was good.

Then God said, "Let us make man in our image, after our likeness; and let them have dominion over the fish of the sea, and over the birds of the air, and over the cattle, and over all the earth, and over every creeping thing that creeps upon the earth." So God created man in his own image, in the image of God he created him; male and female he created them. And God blessed them, and God said to them, "Be fruitful and multiply, and fill the earth and subdue it; and have dominion over the fish of the sea and over the birds of the air and over every living thing that moves upon the earth." And God said, "Behold, I have given you every plant yielding seed which is upon the face of all the earth, and every tree with seed in its fruit; you shall have them for food. And to every beast of the earth, and to every bird of the air, and to everything that has the breath of life, I have given every green plant for food." And it was so. And God saw everything that he had made, and behold, it was very good. And there was evening and there was morning, a sixth day (Gen 1, 24-31).

CHAIRMAN VI: *Display and explain poster.*

Leader:
Thus the heavens and the earth were finished, and all the host of them. And on the seventh day God finished his work which he had done, and he rested on the seventh day from his work which he had done. So God blessed the seventh day and hallowed it, because on it God rested from all his work which he had done in creation (Gen 2, 1-3).

ALL RECITE:
This is our story of the heavens and the earth at their creation.

HYMN: "Praise to the Lord, the Almighty"

II. EARTH'S BEGINNING AND FUTURE

ALL RECITE:
For everything there is a season, and a time
for every matter under heaven:
    a time to be born, and a time to die;
    a time to plant, and a time to pluck
      up what is planted;
    a time to kill, and a time to heal;
    a time to break down, and a time to
      build up;
    a time to weep, and a time to laugh;
    a time to mourn, and a time to dance;
    a time to cast away stones, and a

time to gather stones together;
a time to embrace, and a time to
refrain from embracing;
a time to seek, and a time to lose;
a time to keep, and a time to cast away;
a time to rend, and a time to sew;
a time to keep silence, and a time
to speak;
a time to love, and a time to hate;
a time for war, and a time for peace.
(Ecclesiastes 3: 1-8)

THE FIRST HAPPENING:
And God said, "Let there be light"; and there was light. And God saw that the light was good; and God separated the light from the darkness. God called the light Day, and the darkness he called Night (Gen 1, 3-4).

CHAIRMAN I: *Display and explain poster.*

THE SECOND HAPPENING:
And God said, "Let there be a firmament in the midst of the waters, and let it separate the waters from the waters." And God made the firmament and separated the waters which were under the firmament from the waters which were above the firmament. And it was so. And God called the firmament Heaven (Gen 1, 6-7).

CHAIRMAN II: *Display and explain poster.*

THE THIRD HAPPENING:
And God said, "Let the waters under the heavens be gathered together into one place, and let the dry land appear." And it

was so. God called the dry land Earth, and the waters that were gathered together he called Seas. And God saw that it was good. And God said, "Let the earth put forth vegetation, plants yielding seed, and fruit trees bearing fruit in which is their seed, each according to its kind, upon the earth." And it was so. The earth brought forth vegetation, plants yielding seed according to their own kinds, and trees bearing fruit in which is their seed, each according to its kind (Gen 1, 9-12).

CHAIRMAN III: Display and explain poster, using living plants and various lighting effects.

THE FOURTH HAPPENING:
And God said, "Let there be lights in the firmament of the heavens to separate the day from the night; and let them be for signs and for seasons and for days and years, and let them be lights in the firmament of the heavens to give light upon the earth." And it was so. And God made the two great lights, the greater light to rule the day, and the lesser light to rule the night; he made the stars also. And there was evening and there was morning (Gen 1, 14-16, 19).

CHAIRMAN IV: Display and explain poster and collage.

THE FIFTH HAPPENING:
And God said, "Let the waters bring forth swarms of living creatures, and let birds fly above the earth across the firmament of the heavens." So God created the great sea monsters and every living creature that moves, with which the waters swarm, according to their kinds, and every winged bird according to its kind. And God saw that it was good. And God blessed them, saying, "Be fruitful and multiply and fill the waters in the seas, and let birds multiply on the earth" (Gen 1, 20-22).

CHAIRMAN V: Display and explain poster.

THE SIXTH HAPPENING:
And God said, "Let the earth bring forth living creatures according to their kinds: cattle and creeping things and beasts of the earth according to their kinds." And it was so. Then God said, "Let us make man in our image, after our likeness; and let them have dominion over the fish of the sea, and over the birds of the air, and over the cattle, and over all the earth, and over every creeping thing that creeps upon the earth." So God created man in his own image, in the image of God he created him; male and female he created them. And God blessed them, and God said to them, "Be fruitful and multiply, and fill the earth and subdue it; and have dominion over the fish of the sea and over the birds of the air and over every living thing that moves upon the earth." And God said, "Behold, I have given you every plant yielding seed which is upon the face of the earth, and every tree with seed in its fruit; you shall have them for food. And to every beast of the earth, and to every bird of the air, and to everything that has the breath of life, I have given every green plant for food." And it was so. And God saw everything that he had made, and behold, it was very good (Gen 1, 24, 26-30).

CHAIRMAN VI: Display and explain three-dimensional poster.

LEADER:
Thus the heavens and the earth were finished, and all the host of them (Gen 2, 1).

ALL RECITE:
This is our story; this is our song; that we keep on praising the wonders of God now and in the future.

CLOSING SONG: Play the record, "Turn, Turn, Turn"

THIRD APPROACH:

Making mobiles depicting the six different days of creation.

OBJECTIVES:
1. To teach the students how to creatively work with the different objects they find at home or at school.
2. To foster their awareness that the world depends on God for its existence and that there is a relationship of providence between God and mankind.
3. To increase their realization that they have an important part to play in God's continuing creative act.

MATERIALS:
Iron coat hangers, string, various objects the students can find at home, at school or outdoors for making mobiles.

PROCEDURE:
Divide the class into six groups, each group taking one day of creation and portraying it by means of a mobile. All the mobiles can then be displayed in the classroom and the students can discuss each mobile in detail.

FOURTH APPROACH:

A psychedelic encounter entitled, "Mankind's Need of God and Each Other."

OBJECTIVES:

1. To instill in the students their duty to thank God for creating the world and mankind.

2. To make them aware of their dependence on God for their existence.

3. To challenge them to accept the responsibility they have of helping to make the world a better place in which to live.

MATERIALS:

Strobe lights or color wheels, multi-colored lights, black light, overhead projector, a screen or white sheet, two clear pyrex plates, food coloring, oil, record player, records: "People" (*Barbra Streisand*), "Theme Song from Romeo and Juliet" (*Henry Mancini*), "Circle Game" (*Joni Mitchell*).

PROCEDURE:

The encounter using psychedelic lighting effects can be held in the school hall or the classroom. Appoint two students to act as chairman and co-chairman. With your help they should appoint committees to take care of seating arrangements, decorations, psychedelic lighting and visual effects, music coordination and clean-up. They could also appoint eight students to act as readers. You should begin the encounter by introducing the theme: "Mankind's Need of God and Each Other," and setting the appropriate mood.

The strobe lights or color wheels and the multi-colored lights that flicker on and off at a slow pace will help to enhance a meditative mood in the semi-darkened room. The students could also bring in pictures or photos that depict the beauty of nature to hang around the room. The records such as "People" will bring out the idea that people need other people in order to live truly human and fulfilling lives.

During the playing of the records you can project onto the

white screen or sheet or wall a psychedelic effect produced by using two clear pyrex pie plates over an overhead projector. The bottom plate contains oil and food coloring. You then place the empty pie plate on the other plate and move it in such a way that different designs appear on the screen or sheet or wall. While this is going on the hall or room should be darkened to make the lighting effective in setting the appropriate mood while the record is playing.

The following is a suggested outline of a psychedelic encounter.

Theme: *Mankind's Need of God and Each Other*

Begin by playing the record "People." After the record has been played, the teacher should stress the following point: Because God has made us, we have a responsibility toward one another in making life more meaningful because we have a role to play in God's creative act. We cannot do it alone because God created us to work together in revealing his love to others.

First Reader:
God said, "It is not good that man is alone."

Second Reader:
Man needs other people. He cannot and must not think of himself as separated and independent from everyone else.

Third Reader:
We are all brothers because we all came from the loving hands of the same Creator.

Fourth Reader:
Man is meant to be the master of the things of the world around him.

Fifth Reader:
Man must use these things in a responsible way. Every individual, if he is to survive and fulfill himself, must attempt to break down all the barriers that threaten to prevent people from uniting together. Man must take as his goal not egotistical autonomy but loving communion with all his fellowmen.

Sixth Reader:
Indeed the day will come when men will stand upon what they thought was the most distant star. From there they will move forward into millions of new worlds.

Seventh Reader:
On that day our idea of God will be somewhat less puny and inadequate.

At this point use an overhead projector to show pictures or photos of nature depicting God's beauty and majesty. If possible, these pictures and photos should be brought in by the students themselves. In the background the record "Theme Song from Romeo and Juliet" should be playing.

Eighth Reader:
Let us never forget that this world and everything in it belongs to God.

Then play the record "Circle Game." Stress here the challenge the children have in making this a better world to live in.

Then all recite the following:
Let us look up and live!
God is present in all his glory and majesty!
Let us go and celebrate!

The encounter then concludes with the song "All the Earth Proclaim the Lord."

FIFTH APPROACH:

Creative writing projects.

OBJECTIVES:
1. To give the students the opportunity to seriously reflect upon the type of persons they really are, their inner attitudes and values, their philosophy of life.
2. To encourage the students to express themselves in creative prose or poetry.

MATERIALS:
Notebooks and pencils, color wheels, records for background music.

PROCEDURE:
Have the students think of an inanimate object such as a rock or a tree or a book and then place themselves mentally in this object's place. They should then consider how they would look at life from this object's point of view.

While they are reflecting, the room should be dimly lit with the color wheels in motion to produce a psychedelic effect. Playing some appropriate records as background music will also help to create a reflective mood.

After a suitable period of reflection, have the students write down in a prose or poetry style their personal reflections on how they feel about life. When they have finished, collect the papers and read them to the class and then have a general discussion about the ideas expressed. You may be surprised to see the ideas they will come up with about life, love, death and other subjects.

Here are some samples of statements that students have expressed as a result of this exercise in creative writing:

A BOOK by Alice Sullivan

If there was an object I had to say I was most like, I would have to say I was most like a book. My outside is just the covering, but my inside is what counts. It expresses my feelings. My inside is like the inside of a book in the way that every day of my life is like a new page. Something different happens—maybe not exciting but it's still different.

Sometimes I'm like a book because if you read it a few times it starts to get dull and that's how I am sometimes. Everyone knows what I'm thinking about or knows what I'm going to do next.

LEAVES by Lori Evans

Leaves are living just like man
Because they heard God's command.
They swing in the air and do things we can.
They turn colors like our races
And have shapes like faces.
When they wither on the ground
We can't hear a sound.
But most important of all
Everything is made by God's call,
That makes the big difference of it all.

THE ROAD by David Sedita

Like the road which is always passed upon,
We feel sometimes taken for granted,

Just another individual in a world of individuals.
The road is sometimes abused;
And so are we.
The road is also cared for;
We are also cared for.
A road is added upon;
We grow with each day.
A road accepts things that are done for it;
So we shall accept things that people do for us.
We all live the twisted, upredictable
Road of Life.

A TREE by Cathy Shaw

Did you ever look at a tree? It looks so lonely. No one knows if it is lonely or not. If it were human I wonder how it would feel—sad or happy.

It seems that if a person thinks that no one cares about him he runs away from it all, like maybe by using drugs.

What does a tree do? It can't move. What does it do? I wonder....

A BASKETBALL by Luann Colwell

A basketball is used in a game,
And so is life the same.
The basketball is thrown from person to person,
In a way, so are we.
The way someone may talk about us,
The changing of friends,
Because everyone needs them.
When a basket is made,
It's like we know we've got good friends who care.
We've made a point in the world with someone.
When the air goes out of the basketball,

It's like when we're depressed,
And like the basketball, we're eventually thrown away.

A PRESENT *by Beth Hochreiter*

We are like a present on Christmas morning.
At first we are loved and admired by all.
We are something new and unique.
Because nobody on the whole block received a present like us.
But then we grow older,
And with each year, we are loved less and less.
Or so it seems.
We are soon forgotten about,
No one cares.
We are thrown into the trash.

A COLOR WHEEL *by Kim Gauthier*

It's just like every different color on it is like the personalities of people.

Some are good and some are bad, but we're all equal, but how?

The wheel turns from red to blue to green...we change from good to bad or bad to good, we'll never know....

We're all different, but then again all the same in our ways.

As all the colors meet they change. When we meet different people, we change or they do.

The color wheel is like a person who is all mixed up... they don't know what to do—"Should I have this friend or not?"

The color wheel got made by experimenting; so we should just try, maybe it will work out, maybe it won't, you just gotta wait and see....

A color wheel is different, every color is different. People are different—good, bad, black, white, fat, skinny—yet we're all the same.

We just have to act like ourselves. Don't try to be a big shot if you're not.

Be what you are, not what people make you—just like a color wheel is the way it is.

A STAR *by Lisa Russo*

When a child draws a star,
With its five points,
None can be the same.

Like five people,
Each is different,
Each is separate,
Each is alone.

Every star, like every person,
Has good points,
Has bad points.
Not one is perfect.

A child will take his time,
To draw his star carefully.
It is his masterpiece.

We are God's masterpiece.
We are his stars.
With good and bad points.
His stars that are full of life.
But not one is perfect.

LIGHTS *by Mike Naughton*

People are like lights,
They can be turned on or off.
If the circuit isn't working,
It can't be turned on, it stays off.

If people are alone and without love,
They just can't be turned on.
In a light, when electricity comes to it,
*   it glares out, it is turned on bright.*
In a person, when love comes to him, he can be lit up,
*   glare brightly and be happy.*
The more lights there are, the brighter the room gets.
In the same way, the more love and people there are,
The more happy everyone can be.
Lights come in different colors, shapes and sizes;
*   people do too.*
Even though lights come in different colors,
*   they all give off light.*
People may not live the same way, but we all live
*   for the same purpose—Love and Life.*

THE EARTH AND I by Wayne Heid

As the earth is enriched with fertilizer,
I am enriched with the grace of God.
As the earth is polluted,
I am polluted with evil and temptations.
When there is peace on earth,
I will have peace of mind.
As long as there is life and earth and heaven,
I will have life.
As long as there is love on earth and in heaven.
I will love.

You can readily see from the above examples that this exercise in creative writing gives the students a valuable opportunity to express their innermost feelings and attitudes toward life. The observant teacher can glean many insights about the personalities of her students and therefore be in a better position to guide them to a more fulfilling Christian commitment.

It would also be helpful to the students if several volunteers could neatly type the various poems and essays and illustrate them and make an attractive booklet for the students to keep. This will give them a sense of accomplishment and pride in their work.

As a final activity to summarize what the students have learned about Creation, they could prepare a Mass on the theme of Creation. The following format could be used:

ENTRANCE HYMN: "Shout From the Highest Mountain"

FIRST READING: Genesis 1-2, 3

SECOND READING: Romans 15, 7-13

THIRD READING: John 13, 31-35

To replace the homily or to supplement it, you could present a slide show of pictures of nature which portray God's beauty and majesty. As background music you could play the record "Spirit of God" by the Medical Mission Sisters.

OFFERTORY HYMN: "Of My Hands"

During the Offertory Procession, in addition to bringing the ciborium, wine and water to the altar, the students could bring up various things pertaining to nature, such as twigs, leaves, fruit, pictures of animals, etc.

COMMUNION HYMN: "Lord Who at Thy First Eucharist"

RECESSIONAL HYMN: "Clap Your Hands"

Pentecost

FIRST APPROACH:

Group discussions on the themes: "The Coming of the Holy Spirit," "Freedom and An Invitation," and "No Man is an Island."

OBJECTIVES:

1. To develop in each student the realization that he is important both as an individual and as a member of the Christian community.

2. To enhance group relationships by involving the students in group discussions.

3. To teach the students how to use the Bible as a reference work.

MATERIALS:

Discussion sheets based on the outlines presented here, New Testaments for each member of the class, a record player, the record, "They'll Know We Are Christians by Our Love" (*F.E.L. Publications, Ltd.*); notebooks and pencils.

PROCEDURE:

The readings should be listened to by the class as a group. After each reading there are listed several pivotal questions which should serve as discussion starters, giving the students ideas to help stimulate their discussions. It is preferable to divide the class into small groups for the discussion of the readings and the questions. One person in each group should be chosen to write down the main points of the discussion so that they can be shared later with the whole class.

Discussion Sheet No. 1: "The Coming of the Holy Spirit"

Begin with the reading from the Acts of the Apostles, chapter 2, 1-47. This is the account of the coming of the Holy Spirit.

After the reading, play the record, "They'll Know We Are Christians by Our Love."

Then have one of the students read the following:

> Every individual is challenged to be a witness of his faith to the entire community in which he lives and works and plays. He does this by following the example of Christ and being a man of love, compassion and justice to everyone he meets, whether a member of his own family, a neighbor, or a stranger in need of help.
>
> As members of Christ's mystical body, it is we who must bring Christ's redemptive love and grace to people who are searching for redemption, for forgiveness, for meaning in their lives. This means being genuinely concerned about others, really caring for others, not only in words but also in deeds.

PIVOTAL QUESTIONS:

1. When other people look at us today will they be able to see the meaning of the song "They'll Know We Are Christians by Our Love" reflected in our lives? What are some practical ways we can show we are Christians by our love?

2. The Holy Spirit who is present in each one of us today is the same Holy Spirit who inspired the early Christians. Why aren't we spreading the Christian gospel with the same zeal that the apostles and early Christians had?

Discussion Sheet No. 2: "Freedom and An Invitation"

First Reading:
If a man is truly free, he is free in the depths of his heart and spirit. When we lack freedom, it's mostly because we are enslaved by fear. Fear itself has no power to destroy our freedom, but often we allow our fears to take control of us, to stifle our creativity and imagination, to cramp our life-style. As long as we ourselves give in to fear and whatever else restricts our freedom, no other person can set us free. It is something we have to overcome ourselves. We need courage to step out of the unhealthy boundaries that restrict us, and to give our imaginations a chance to wander and dream and set goals for us to conquer. We need to overcome our fear of the darkness, the unknown, the unsure, and take the leap into freedom, guided always by the liberating powers of faith and prayer.

"Do not be conformed to this world but be transformed by the renewal of your mind, that you may prove what is the will of God, what is good and acceptable and perfect" (Rom 12:2).

PIVOTAL QUESTIONS:
1. Why is freedom so important in man's life?
2. What are some obstacles to freedom in my life? How can I overcome them?
3. How does the right use of freedom help me to get out of myself and think of the welfare of others?

Second Reading:
Christ, by his death and resurrection, offers us a challenge

to give a new direction to our lives, to go beyond the shallowness and superficiality of everyday life and to consider the deeper meaning of life and death.

Christ has given us the ultimate answer to the mysteries of life and death. By his life he has shown us that love must be the guiding force in our relationships with ourselves, with our neighbors and with God. By his glorious resurrection from the dead he has given us assurance that death is not only the end of earthly life, but more importantly, the beginning of eternal life.

Christ therefore offers us a chance to live a new life, to break out of our limited, earthly vision and set our sights on eternal life. Through this Christian outlook we will lead more fulfilling lives and be of greater service to our fellowmen.

"I am the resurrection and the life; he who believes in me, though he die, yet shall he live, and whoever lives and believes in me shall never die" (John 11, 25-26).

PIVOTAL QUESTIONS:

1.   What kind of freedom does Christ offer to those who follow him?

2.   In what sense can we look upon physical death as a liberation?

3.   What meaning should the Resurrection have for our personal lives?

Discussion Sheet No. 3: "No Man is An Island"

First Reading:

No man can "go it alone" in this life. Man by nature is a social being and there is a deep bond of dependency uniting all human beings. That is one reason why Christ founded a Church to be his Chosen People, a community where each one would be attentive to and care for the needs of his fellow men.

As members of the Church, we have a community among all men, but especially among those people with whom we come in contact every day—our family, friends, classmates, teachers and fellow parishioners. As members of the Church we are all members of God's family, God's Chosen People. Therefore we must strive to be friendly and harmonious in all our interpersonal relationships. We are responsible in many ways for the salvation of each other. We are to be channels of Christ's love and grace to each other.

PIVOTAL QUESTIONS:

1. Why does man feel the need to belong to a human community and the Christian community?

2. How does being a Christian affect our relationships with our fellowmen?

3. In what ways are we responsible for each other's salvation?

Second Reading:

The best place where we can most effectively carry out our mission of building community is the Church during the eucharistic celebration of the Mass. This is when the People of God are most united in faith and love, and witness to the presence of Christ in each other. The Church is a community of men who share the same spirit and the same faith and strengthen their bonds of community through prayer. It is this faith community which is a continuing sign to the world that God is ever-present among his people.

PIVOTAL QUESTIONS:

1. Why should men be committed to each other's welfare?

2. How can Christians be a continuing sign of God's presence in the world?

3. In what way is the Eucharist the center of our Christian lives?

SECOND APPROACH:

Making collages on the theme: "Christian Community—Social Community"

OBJECTIVES:
1. To help the students to become more aware of people outside of their specific Christian community.
2. To make them realize their importance as dedicated individuals in both their social and Christian communities.
3. To challenge them to come up with ideas on how they can put into practice in their social community the principles and ideals they learn in their Christian community.

MATERIALS:
At least a day or two before they are going to make their collages, ask the students to bring in magazines, newspapers, pictures, scissors, glue and any other materials they will need to make their collages.

PROCEDURE:
Divide the class into groups of four. Tell them that their collages should portray the various ways they can help build a better social community by putting into practice the principles, ideals and moral values they learn in their Christian community.

When all of the collages have been made, have each group present their collage and explain it to the entire class. A general discussion could follow.

THIRD APPROACH:

A dramatic presentation of the Pentecost event entitled, "You Are There."

OBJECTIVES:
 1.   To introduce the students to dramatic role-playing.
 2.   To get them involved in using the New Testament as a resource material.
 3.   To teach them the effective use of audio-visual aids.
 4.   To instill in them a greater awareness of their faith and the responsibility they have to spread it.

MATERIALS:
New Testament, 8mm. movie camera, tape recorder, costumes (if feasible).

PROCEDURE:
 Explain to the students that you would like them to re-enact the New Testament account of the coming of the Holy Spirit.
 First they will have to read the account as it is presented in the Acts of the Apostles, chapter 2, 1-47. When they have finished reading the account, ask them to play out the account in a dramatic presentation. Twelve boys can be selected to portray the Apostles and one girl to play the Blessed Mother. One boy or girl could play the role of a traveling reporter along with a partner to follow him or her with a movie camera. The reporter could ask the students who will be acting as the crowd of bystanders such questions as: "Do you think these men are drunk?" "What is this 'spirit' that they are preaching about?" If it is feasible, costumes could be used to enhance the dramatization.
 Also, if it is possible, the students could arrange to show the completed movie to their parents or to other classes in the school.

FOURTH APPROACH:

A Bible Service on the theme: "By Our Actions We Are Known."

OBJECTIVES:
   1.   To combine a learning situation with a prayerful experience.
   2.   To remind the students of the special role they play in society as Christians.
   3.   To give them the incentive to profess their faith more actively and courageously.

MATERIALS:
A Bible, two candles, a small table or desk, Bible Service sheets for each student based on the outline presented here.

PROCEDURE:
   The Bible Service should be held in the classroom. The Bible, flanked by two lit candles, should be opened on a table in the front of the room. The table could be decorated with a banner.
   A leader should be chosen to conduct the service and a boy and a girl could act as readers. The following is a suggested outline:

Bible Service: "By Our Actions We Are Known"

Leader:
Lord, how does one learn to pray?

First Reader:
He learns with his flesh and blood.

Second Reader:
He learns with his eyes and his hands.

First Reader:
He learns with his heart.

All:
But what does this have to do with us?

Leader:
Because God made you, you are very important to him. Your responsibility to him is to bring others back to him by your actions.

Second Reader:
A Christian should be known by his actions and his getting involved in helping people.

All:
Then it is high time we start making happy noises about God, that we boldly proclaim his name and shout his praises.

At this point the students could display the collages they made in the second approach, depicting the various ways in which they could be of service in their social community.

Conclude the service by having all of the students join in the singing of "Whatsoever You Do."

FIFTH APPROACH:

A prayer ceremony entitled: "Let Us Break Bread Together."

OBJECTIVES:

1. To encourage the students to extend their friendship in a practical way to others outside of their community who may need love and friendship.

2. To make them more aware of others who live in culturally deprived areas.

3. To show them the meaning of Christian love and service.

MATERIALS:

Prayer sheets based on the outline presented below, a loaf (or loaves depending on the size of the group) of Italian or French bread, small table(s), two lit candles.

PROCEDURE:

Arrange for a class from a school in an underprivileged area to spend a morning or afternoon at your school with your class acting as hosts. The idea is to get the students to meet and share their experiences and then take part in a breaking-of-the-bread ceremony. Invite a priest or deacon to conduct the prayer service. If he cannot attend you can perform it yourself. Ask one of the students to do the reading during the ceremony.

Before the ceremony begins, explain to the students that since they have come together and shared their ideas and different experiences, they can express their friendship by breaking bread together. This will then set the basis for explaining the meaning of the Eucharist as the sacramental breaking of bread which symbolizes the bonds of friendship which unite the members of the Church with each other and with God.

LET US BREAK BREAD TOGETHER

ENTRANCE HYMN: "Here We Are"

Celebrant:
Father, here we are all friends expressing our unity and friend-ship by gathering together at this table to share a meal and to give you thanks.

In silence each person takes a piece of bread from the celebrant and then all recite:
"I am the bread of life; he who comes to me shall not hunger and he who believes in me shall never thirst. But I said to you that you have seen me and yet do not believe. All the Father gives me will come to me; and him who comes to me I will not cast out. For I have come down from heaven, not to do my own will, but the will of him who sent me" (Jn 6:35-38).

Then all eat the bread and recite together:
This bread that we have just eaten is ordinary bread, the same that we eat at home. But we do know that there is another bread, the Bread of Life.

Then all stand and listen to the reading of the Word of God (Jn 6:53-58).

After a brief period of reflection, all recite:
The love that others show us makes us want to love them too and be ourselves. It is when we think of God who gave us his only son as the bread of life that we begin to see the true love of him who made us. Therefore, we should have greater love for each other and show it each day.

At this point have all the children form a circle and have each one extend the greeting of peace with a word of kindness to the person on his or her right.

CLOSING HYMN: "They'll Know We Are Christians By Our Love"

Advent

FIRST APPROACH:

Group discussion on the theme: "The Coming of the Lord."

OBJECTIVES:
1. To acquaint the students with the Old and New Testament prophets who were waiting for the coming of the Messiah. For many this was their lifetime dream.
2. To give them a deeper understanding of why the Church celebrates the Advent season.

MATERIALS:
Bibles and discussion sheets listing various Old and New Testament prophecies concerning the coming of the Messiah, notebooks and pencils.

PROCEDURE:
Begin the class with the song: "The King of Glory."
Then distribute the sheets listing the Old and New Testament quotations proclaiming the coming of the Messiah. Here are a few examples:

"For to us a child is born, to us a son is given; and the government will be upon his shoulder, and his name will be called 'Wonderful Counselor, Mighty God, Everlasting Father, Prince of Peace.' Of the increase of his government and of peace there will be no end, upon the throne of David, and over his kingdom, to establish it, and to uphold it with justice and with righteousness from this time forth and for evermore. The zeal of the Lord of hosts will do this" (Is 9, 6-8).

"This is the Messiah whom the Most High has kept until the end of days, who will arise from the posterity of David, and will come and speak to them; he will denounce them for their wickedness, and will cast up before them their contemptuous dealings. For first he will set them living before his judgment seat, and when he has reproved them, then he will destroy them. But he will deliver in mercy the remnant of my people, those who have been saved throughout my borders, and he will make them joyful until the end comes, the day of judgment, of which I spoke to you at the beginning" (Esd 2, 32-34).

"And then they will see the Son of man coming in clouds with great power and glory. And then he will send out the angels, and gather his elect from the four winds, from the ends of the earth to the ends of heaven" (Mk 13, 26-27).

The following are the words of John the Baptist:

"I baptize you with water for repentance, but he who is coming after me is mightier than I, whose sandals I am not worthy to carry; he will baptize you with the Holy Spirit and with fire. His winnowing fork is in his hand, and he will clear his threshing floor and gather his wheat into the granary, but the chaff he will burn with unquenchable fire" (Mt 3, 11-12).

Then explain to the students that they should read these quotations over very carefully and try to detect the Jewish people's mood of uncertainty or anxiety since they really didn't know whom they should look for as the Messiah.

Tell them to look for more quotations in the Bible which denote the same mood of uncertainty as well as the feeling that the people were looking for someone to be their ruler. Then the class should break up into small groups to discuss their research findings. At the end of the discussion period, which should last for about twenty minutes, the representatives from each group should present their findings to the entire class.

As a final exercise to summarize their findings, each group should take one quotation and illustrate it by making a banner or a diorama.

SECOND APPROACH:

Composition writing on the theme: "Guess Who's Coming to Dinner!"

OBJECTIVES:

1. To enhance creative writing and thought-provoking ideas.

2. To encourage class participation as well as group work.

3. To foster the students' awareness that they too are an "awaiting people" just like the people in the Old Testament.

MATERIALS:
Notebooks and pencils.

PROCEDURE:
Explain to the students that they are to write a composition

on the following theme: "Guess Who's Coming to Dinner!" Tell them to imagine that they have just received a phone call or telegram from Christ informing them that he is coming to their house for Christmas dinner and will spend a few days with them after the holidays. After they have reflected on this for a suitable period of time have them write down their reactions and what preparations they would make for his coming and what special gift they would give him. Here are a few actual samples of what some students wrote:

If Christ called me I think I'd be quite stunned. I would wonder why he chose to call me out of the millions of other people in the world. For I am not the most studious or agreeable person.

After his call I would probably tell my whole family and ask for their help to prepare for this great coming. First I would clean the whole house top to bottom so it would be fit for Christ to live in and then I would bake our favorite foods such as chocolate chip cookies, homemade bread and many others. I would also put my record albums away for they are quite noisy.

After Christ's arrival we would sit down and have a long talk about many different things. When it was time to eat we would sit down, give praise to the Father, and break and pass the holy wafers.

As soon as we were through we would spend a quiet evening enjoying the Christmas carolers who would come by the house every so often. In the middle of our little conversation I would bring Christ my token of gratitude—a homemade candle. We would then end the day attending midnight Mass. I know that I would never forget this day in my whole life.
—Peggyann Griscavage

If someone sent me a telegram saying he was Christ and was coming over to my house for the holidays, I would say it was just a prank or some goofball. But if I had some kind of knowledge that it was really Jesus, I would prepare for his coming. First of all our family would clean the house so that it would look immaculate. Second, we would put up decorations for the occasion. Third, my mother would prepare special food that we could eat for the celebration of his coming to our house. And finally we would anxiously wait until he was at our doorstep.

—Stanley Koreyva'

Unbelievable was the slip of paper that arrived in the mail just a minute ago. Jesus, yes Jesus, had sent me a letter asking to be a guest at my house!

Thinking of it as a prank pulled by some of my envious "friends" I rushed the beautifully written letter to my mom who was knitting a pair of socks for my dad. But both to my and her amazement, all she saw was a blank piece of paper while I unmistakably saw three sentences.

But I just put it out of my head until Christmas Eve. My parents left to do some Christmas shopping while I sat curiously watching a television program. The very second the program was over, an unbelievably shining light fell on the door. Anxious but afraid, I opened it and, as silence fell on the earth, I spotted Jesus who was dressed in white with his face shining like a light. Falling on my knees, I kissed his feet and said, "Lord, I am a sinner and not worthy to even lay eyes upon you."

But with his hand stretched out, I held it and rose. Seeing that I was afraid he said, "Child, I am with you. You have nothing to fear."

It was approximately two hours that we just sat and talked without pressure of time. His story wasn't long but one second of speaking to him contained more knowledge than what I learned in twelve years. My last question was, "What is heaven

like?" *Giving me a sudden stare he said, "Being good and holy on earth can only answer your question." With that he left, leaving me stunned and living in a dream.*
—Jane Cychowski

If someone called me claiming to be Christ I would think he was a nut. I'd have the number traced and I'd ask if it were a collect call. After I was convinced it was Christ I'd get down to business. I would ask him what day he would come and at what time. Then I would really clean the house.

When Christ would arrive, I'd pass out. Weird, way out, it would be unbelievable! But I'd treat him as a man not a God.
—M. Wasielewski

I would prepare for Christ's coming by inviting some of my friends over for a home Mass. When Christ comes I'll show him how much I love him and share him with my friends. The gift I would give him is the gift of thanks—that is, thanking him for everything he has given me, especially my wonderful parents. I will offer him my home for as long as he wishes to stay.
—Margaret Bracken

If Christ came to visit me, the preparations that I would make would be: First, even though the house is very clean, I'd still go over it. Next, I would prepare a dinner. I would invite a few of my friends. Before dinner, we will all sit in a circle and have a shared prayer experience. Then we would have dinner and a social conversation. If I were to give Christ a gift, it would probably be a car or some clothing.
—Stephen Bigotto

If Christ called and told me that he was coming to visit me, the first thing I would do would be to go to confession. Then

I'll make sure that everything in my house is in perfect order. I would buy him a nice big juicy steak and cook the steak his favorite way and keep my fingers crossed that all will turn out okay.

—Kathy Gaul

There was a knock at the door. When I opened it there he was—Christ. I immediately started to prepare dinner for him. During and after dinner we talked until Jesus said that he must be about his Father's business. I told him that I must give him a gift before he left. I know that money doesn't mean much to him so I promised that I would try to be a better Christian by loving and sharing more with my neighbors.

—John Ruane

It is easy to see from these samples that a teacher can learn a lot about students' attitudes toward Jesus. They can be very revealing.

A good project to conclude this activity would be to have the students neatly type out the compositions, illustrate them and make them into an attractive booklet for each student to keep.

THIRD APPROACH:

A presentation and discussion of the filmstrip "The Advent Liturgy" (Thomas S. Klise Co., P.O. Box 3418, Peoria, Ill. 61414). This filmstrip emphasizes faith in the Christ of the first Christmas, hope in the Christ of the Second Coming, and charity toward the Christ we meet daily in one another.

MATERIALS:
Filmstrip, projector, notebooks and pencils, discussion questions.

OBJECTIVES:

1.   To enable the students to relate Christ of the first Christmas with Christ of the Second Coming (Parousia).

2.   To foster their awareness that they should see Christ in others.

3.   To enhance class participation through group discussions and group cooperation in making mobiles.

PROCEDURE:

Show the filmstrip to the entire class as a group. Then have the class break up into groups of four. Each group should discuss the following points based on their observations from viewing the filmstrip:

1.   Compare the faith of the people of the Old Testament with the hope of the people of the New Testament concerning Christ's coming.

2.   How can we show charity toward the "Christ" we meet daily in one another?

After a suitable period of discussion, each group should express and summarize their discussion ideas by making mobiles depicting:

a.   the faith of the people of the Old Testament.

b.   the hope of the people of the New Testament.

c.   various ways in which they can show charity toward their fellowmen.

A representative from each group could display and discuss with the entire class the meaning of his group's mobiles.

FOURTH APPROACH:

An exercise in creative writing in which the students rewrite in their own words those biblical psalms which reflect the joy of the people as they expectantly await the coming of their Messiah.

MATERIALS:
Notebooks and pencils.

OBJECTIVES:
1. To make the students more acutely aware of the joy that the people of the Old Testament experienced as a result of the expectation that their Messiah was coming to save them.
2. To encourage them to express their own joy as they await Christ's coming.
3. To interest them in the use of the Bible as a reference source.

PROCEDURE:
Begin the exercise by pointing out to the students several examples of psalms which reflect the people's joy and confidence that Yahweh will send them a savior. Psalm 33 (34), for example, looks upon and praises God as the protector of his people. Psalm 56 (57) depicts the people's confidence in God as their deliverer.

Then have them look for other psalms which express these and similar themes and tell them that you want them to rewrite in their own words the psalms they choose, to express their own personal confidence and joy in Christ's coming. Here are a few examples of what can be done in a creative writing exercise like this:

PSALM 12 (13)

Lord, don't forget me for what I have done. Stay with me.
Dear God, you have a right to be angry. I have gone against you

in order to save myself. There is sorrow in my heart, in my soul. Why have I done it? Don't I love you? Help me! Do not make me blind to the light of you. Teach me to rejoice in your salvation. So give me hope. Give me another chance. I will try. Save me, Lord. I want to sing of your goodness.

—Lisa Russo

PSALM 72 (73)

God is good to those who are honest. Everyone is envious of the wicked because they see them grow wealthy.

The wicked act like they have no pain or no earthly burdens. Pride adorns them as much as violence. They curse and threaten other men and when you tell them God is watching, they say, "How does God know?"

They are carefree in what they do and are always increasing in wealth. It is hard to remain an innocent man because of all the temptations. Clean-hearted people suffer every day by trying to do what is right.

The wicked do not believe they are wasting lives by their criminal ways. They can do what they please but God will judge them.

—Robert Walsh

PSALM 13 (14)

Oh my God, only fools have said:
There is no God, alive or dead.
These fools are corrupt, they do no good.
They wouldn't love, even if they could.
Does any among us understand?
Do we seek God, I do not know.
You, Lord Almighty, look down upon us.
We, the children of men, have but one desire:
We long to dwell in your fortress,

To love you and forget all the distress.
We love you, though it may not show.
We try our best, I think you know.
—Lynda Smith

PSALM 48 (49)

All you people listen to me! Evil is no good. Evil destroys all good and gets you nowhere. When you die you leave behind everything. You can't take it with you. But the good shall thrive over evil. They shall take peace with them to their grave. People who are really rich, you shall have nothing left till you have loved and shared your good fortune. Your houses, servants and riches mean nothing to God in heaven for he considers you equal to those less fortunate than yourself. If you believe in God you won't fear evil and will live in peace forever.
—Laura Knittel

PSALM 64 (65)

Oh Lord, we were blessed by having healthy limbs that enabled us to be the number one basketball team. We want to keep it that way and we can because we are all healthy, but at times we take advantage of it. Nobody stopped to thank you for any of this, but I'm sure they are all thankful for all you have done for them.

—Danny Lynd

PSALM 13 (14)

Oh God, you keep saying you will come back down to earth and choose the wise and good. But dear God, no one is wise and good; everyone makes mistakes sometime in their lives. There are also failures and successes in this mad world. So no one is wise and good. Not me or anyone. Help us, please.

PSALM 11 (12)

Oh Lord, help those people who feel they are great but really are not. Help those who act falsely toward their friends and neighbors. Don't forget them or me. We all try to do our best although it comes out wrong. Help us and don't forget us.

—Cathy Shaw

PSALM 17 (18)

Oh Lord, you have helped me when I've had problems and I overcame them. Thank you. You made me safe from my enemies and I now know that I must pray for them to be better. Many times they made fun of me, especially when I made mistakes. They forgot that they made mistakes also. You helped me to ignore them. Now they don't bother me any more. I really want to belong.

—Mary Landers

PSALM 24 (25)

To you, man in the sky, I bring my life. In you, God, I put my trust. Don't let the other gangs clobber and humiliate me. I will wait for you on the corner for no one shall touch me! The others will damn themselves while drinking and shooting. They shall be laid waste in shame. Oh Lord, let me walk your road. Let me hear your words to mold myself. Lord, you have done this for all, but few follow. Lord, show me your way.

—Jeffrey Kilker

These examples serve to illustrate the latent, creative thoughts toward God and prayer which the students can express in writing and which will give the perceptive teacher different ideas on how to cultivate the students' prayer life more effective-ly.

Again, it would be good to have the students neatly type out their psalms, illustrate them, and make them into attractive and useful prayer booklets.

Incarnation

FIRST APPROACH:

A Bible Vigil on the theme: "God Became Man in Christ."

OBJECTIVES:

1. To foster in the students a deeper awareness and appreciation of the fact that Christ, by becoming man, has thereby raised the dignity of mankind.

2. To give them a better understanding of the Virgin birth.

3. To develop a better understanding of the Bible and a greater appreciation of its beauty.

MATERIALS:

Crib scene, spot light, Bible Vigil sheets.

PROCEDURE:

Set up the crib scene in the middle of the room with the spot light shining on it. Have the students arrange their desks in a circle around the crib scene. Distribute the Bible Vigil sheets and appoint five students to take the parts of leaders and readers. The following outline could be used:

Bible Vigil: "God Became Man in Christ."

OPENING HYMN: "Silent Night"

Leader I:
"For to us a child is born, to us a son is given; and the government will be upon his shoulder, and his name will be called 'Wonderful Counselor, Mighty God, Everlasting Father, Prince of Peace'" (Is 9, 6).

Leader II:
"Of the increase of this government and of peace there will be no end, upon the throne of David, and over his kingdom, to establish it, and to uphold it with justice and with righteousness from this time forth and for evermore" (Is 9, 7).

Reader I:
We believe, dear God, that this was made possible by a woman of Nazareth.

Reader II:
She is truly the mother of God; but at the same time she is a virgin.

Reader III:
As the angel told her at the Annunciation: "The Holy Spirit will come upon you, and the power of the Most High will overshadow you; therefore the child to be born will be called holy, the Son of God" (Lk 1, 35).

Leader I:
At Christmas the shepherds and the magi saw Christ with their own eyes—they could touch and embrace him.

Leader II:
The rest of us live also in the flesh and believe even though we could not see or touch him.

Reader I:
We know that his incarnation is continued in a visible Church made up of human beings.

Reader II:
We know that he is living for us in the sacraments.

Reader III:
But best of all, we know, believe and hope that at the end of all time all of us will see our Savior in his glorified body.

All:
This is our hope, this is our wish.

CONCLUDING HYMN: "To Jesus Christ, Our Sovereign King"

SECOND APPROACH:

A dramatic program entitled, "Christmas Around the World."

OBJECTIVES:
    1.   To develop in the students an awareness and appreciation of the various ways people of other countries observe Christmas.
    2.   To enhance group participation through research and dramatics.

MATERIALS:
Encyclopedias or other reference books, materials for making costumes.

PROCEDURE:
Divide the class into groups of four or five. Explain to them that each group should choose a country on which they would like to do research concerning various Christmas customs and observances. Each group would then prepare a song, dance or skit portraying the different customs and observances of the country they chose which they can present to the entire class. If it is feasible, they could make costumes reflecting the native dress of the various countries. The songs, dances and skits could also be presented to the other classes in the school. Perhaps their parents could be invited to attend.

THIRD APPROACH:

Hosting a Christmas Party for first graders of an inner city school.

OBJECTIVES:
1.   To make the students more aware that there are children in their neighborhood who are less fortunate than they are.
2.   To help them to extend themselves outside of their own community by sharing with others in need.
3.   To enhance class spirit and morale by group cooperation in a common project.

MATERIALS:
Invitations, refreshments, gifts, Santa Claus costume, Christmas tree, decorations.

PROCEDURE:

The Christmas party should be held in the school hall if possible. Appoint a chairman and co-chairman. They in turn should set up different committees to take care of the invitations, refreshments, decorations, entertainment, gifts and clean-up. Perhaps the girls could bake some cookies or cakes and the boys could be responsible for the drinks. Also, let them decide whether they want to buy gifts or make them themselves. One of the boys should be chosen to play Santa Claus.

This party-activity will not only benefit the needy children for whom it is being conducted. The students themselves will enjoy acting as hosts and gift-givers. They will learn the valuable lesson that love means caring for other people and that it is better to give than to receive.

FOURTH APPROACH:

A creative project entitled, "The Christmas Tree of Symbols."

OBJECTIVES:

1. To summarize the students' accomplishments and studies during the Advent season.

2. To give the students an opportunity to give witness to the good deeds they performed for others during Advent.

MATERIALS:

Christmas tree, various objects to symbolize the students' good deeds.

PROCEDURE:

Explain to the students that instead of decorating the

Christmas tree with the traditional lights and ornaments, they should decorate it with various objects which symbolize the good acts they performed during the weeks of Advent in preparation for the birth of Christ. For example, a small toy broom to symbolize that someone swept the kitchen floor, or some cooking utensil to portray that when someone's mother was ill, the student cooked dinner for the family, or a baby bottle could be hung to symbolize that one of the students baby sat for someone in need.

This activity hopefully will teach the students group cooperation and the true meaning of Advent and Christmas: the giving of self to God and fellowman in preparation for the coming of Christ.

Eucharist

FIRST APPROACH:

A group discussion based on the filmstrip "The Eucharist: Bond of Love" (Alba House Communications, Canfield, Ohio 44406). This fast-moving presentation clearly shows the relation between liturgy and life, explaining the Eucharist as a covenant of love between God and his people.

OBJECTIVES:

1. To enable the students to see the comparison between the Passover Meal and the Last Supper.

2. To enable them to understand the Eucharistic meal within the context of a family meal.

3. To make them more aware of the sanctity and unity of the family.

4. To instill a greater appreciation of their own families and the family of the Christian community.

MATERIALS:

The sound filmstrip "The Eucharist: Bond of Love," discussion sheets based on the questions found in the discussion guide accompanying the filmstrip, Bibles, notebooks and pencils.

PROCEDURE:

Before showing the filmstrip, give some introductory remarks stressing the fact that the Eucharist is a communal celebration of life and unity found in the love expressed within the family and the community. Emphasize the need for solidarity within the community and the importance of reaching out to others as a faith-response to this communal bond of love.

Also stress the idea that Christ is present to us in the Eucharist under the appearance of bread which is offered to all and shared by all. Mention the rite of the "breaking of the bread" which was the early Christians' name for the Eucharist and which signifies the sharing aspect of the Eucharist. The Eucharist is not only a meal shared by brothers but a meal shared with Christ.

It would also be appropriate here to have the students read the Gospel accounts of the Last Supper (Mt 26, 17-29; Mk 14, 12-25; Lk 22, 7-23; Jn 13, 1-35) and compare them with the Old Testament Passover story (Ex 12, 1-51).

After this preliminary introduction, show the filmstrip to the entire class. After the filmstrip, pass out the discussion sheets. The discussion guide which accompanies the filmstrip can provide the pivotal questions for the discussion. The class should be divided into small groups. One person in each group should write down the main points discussed so that he can give an oral report to the entire class.

Also contained in the discussion guide is an outline for a celebration of the Eucharist which uses the filmstrip as the homily. If feasible, an evening Mass based on the outline could be held in one of the student's homes. This would clearly illustrate the connection between the Eucharistic meal and the family meal.

SECOND APPROACH:
A dramatization combining elements of a Passover Seder Service
and the Last Supper of Christ with his apostles.

OBJECTIVES:
 1. To point out to the students the similarities between
the Old Testament Passover Meal and the New Testament
Last Supper.
 2. To foster in them a greater awareness and appreciation
of their Jewish heritage.

MATERIALS:
Seven festival candles, paper cups, plates and napkins for each
student, several bottles of wine (or grape juice), three matzohs
for each student, several bowls of bitter herbs, charoseth (a mixture of finely chopped apples, nuts and cinnamon mixed with a
little wine), salt water, a Bible, Passover Seder Service sheets
for each student based on the outline below.

PROCEDURE:
 It would be more convenient to conduct this service in the
school dining hall. Each student should have a paper cup, plate
and napkin. In the middle of the main table between the seven
festival candles there should be a napkin, plate and cup full of
wine or grape juice reserved in honor of Elijah to commemorate
the Jewish tradition that Elijah comes back to his people on Passover Eve at the Seder dinner.
 There should be three matzohs for each student and enough
wine or grape juice to fill each student's cup four times during
the service. Depending on the number of students, there should
be several bowls of bitter herbs, charoseth and salt water.

Distribute the Seder Sheets to each student. The teacher should read the leader's part and twelve students should be chosen to act as readers.

The following format could be used for the Passover Service:

A PASSOVER SEDER SERVICE

1.   BLESSING THE FESTIVAL CANDLES

Leader: According to an ancient Jewish custom, it is the task of the mother to light the festival lights in every service which takes place in the Jewish home. To us, this gesture symbolizes the coming of Christ, the Messiah, the Light of the world. The solemn blessing of light at the Easter vigil service finds its origin in this Jewish custom, which also reminds us of the lighted candles upon the altar, the table of our daily Eucharistic banquet.

Passover is the Jewish festival of freedom. In this spring season of the year the Hebrews of old were liberated from slavery in Egypt. We bless these candles because these lights stand for our hope that one day all men all over the world will gain their freedom. (*Light the candles*).

All recite Psalm 36, 7-10:
How precious is thy steadfast love, O God!
The children of men take refuge in the shadow
of thy wings.
They feast on the abundance of thy house, and
thou givest them drink from the river of thy delights.
For with thee is the fountain of life; in thy light
do we see light.

O continue thy steadfast love to those who know
thee; and thy salvation to the upright of heart!

Leader: Praised be Thou, O Lord, our God. Who has
made us holy and commanded us to light the Sabbath and festival lights.

All: (*Repeat as above.*)

Leader: Praised be Thou, O Lord, our God. Who has given
us life and brought us to this festival day of joyful celebration.
Amen.

All: (*Repeat as above.*)

2. PRAYER OVER THE WINE (Kiddush).

All recite Psalm 104: 1a, 10-15, 1a:
Bless the Lord, O my soul! O Lord my God,
thou art very great!
Thou makest springs gush forth in the valleys;
they flow between the hills, they give drink to every beast
of the field; the wild asses quench their thirst.
By them the birds of the air have their habitation;
they sing among the branches.
Thou dost cause the grass to grow for the cattle, and
plants for man to cultivate, that he may bring forth food from
the earth, and wine to gladden the heart of man.
Bless the Lord, O my soul! O Lord my God,
thou art very good!

All recite together:
O Lord our God, out of love You have given us many days

of joy and holidays of gladness. We thank Thee for this festival of Passover, which reminds us of the Hebrew story of freedom. The matzoh that we eat is a symbol that we too share in the history of the Jewish people as our fathers did in every age. We too shall serve God in holiness and help all people who are in need.

Leader: Praised be Thou, O Lord our God, Ruler of the world, who has created the fruit of the vine. Amen.

All: (*Repeat as above.*)

Leader: Here we recall Christ's words to his apostles at the Last Supper: "Take this, and divide it among yourselves; for I tell you that from now on I shall not drink of the fruit of the vine until the kingdom of God comes" (Lk 22, 17, 18).

(*Everyone now drinks the First Cup.*)

Leader: At this point in the Passover Meal there took place the traditional washing of hands. The washing of hands during the Passover Meal symbolized the interior cleansing necessary for those partaking in the ritual—just as does the celebrant's act of washing his hands during Mass. It was probably at this point in the ritual that Christ washed the feet of his disciples as an expression of his new commandment of love and to show the dignity of service in the new law (Jn 13, 2-15).

3. PRAYER OVER THE HERBS

Reader No. 1: Passover is celebrated in the spring of the year. After the winter, nature starts its work again with God's blessing. The fields are clothed in beauty, as new flowers and plants start to grow. Let us bless the new food that comes from the good earth. (*Dip parsley in salt water, then eat it.*)

Leader: We thank Thee, O Lord, our God, for the fresh food that grows from the verdant earth. Amen.

All: (Repeat as above.)

4. BREAKING OF THE BREAD

Leader (*Breaks matzoh in half, hides part for end of meal, then reads*):
This is the bread of trouble that our families ate in the land of Egypt. May all who are hungry come and eat. May all who are in need come and celebrate Passover with us. This year some people are suffering like slaves. Next year may everybody be free. (*Everyone eats half of the matzoh*).

5. THE FOUR QUESTIONS:

Readers No. 2, 3, 4, 5 and 6:
2. Why is this night different from all other nights?
3. a) Why on this night do we eat matzoh?
4. b) Why do we hold this special Seder service?
5. c) Why do we dip twice; once in salt water and once in charoseth?
6. d). Why on this night do we eat bitter herbs?

All sing the hymn: "Lord, Who Throughout These Forty Days"

6. THE ANSWER

Reader No. 2: We celebrate Passover because our ancestors were freed from slavery in Egypt. Jewish people have retold this story for thousands of years. God wants human beings to be free, but evil rulers like Pharoah refused to obey God's command. Passover teaches that freedom is the most precious possession in life.

7. THE FOUR SONS

Reader No. 3: The story of Passover may be told in many ways. The wise child loves his parents and is eager to learn from his teachers. He asks earnest questions about the customs of the festival, especially at the Seder. To him, we answer with love: "This service is held in order to worship the Lord our God; to thank Him for our freedom and for all the good things of life."

Reader No. 4: The wicked child misbehaves at home, at school, and in the synagogue. He is selfish and does not believe in the rights of other people. He must be warned that he will not be accepted in the company of free men because he does not respect the story of freedom and its beautiful ceremonies.

Reader No. 5: The simple child would like to know what Passover means. So he says: "What is this all about?" Answer him kindly: "Passover is important because of what God did for us when our people went forth out of Egypt."

Reader No. 6: The shy child should be treated with patience. It is our religious duty to befriend him and to tell him why we celebrate the Passover holiday.

All sing the hymn: "Praise to the Lord, the Almighty"

All recite together:
We are all wise children. We love the story of Passover. We thank God for all the miracles that led to the freedom of Israel from Egyptian bondage. We thank God for the Sabbath and all the wonderful holidays in our religion. We thank God for the Torah. We are grateful for all God's gifts. For each we say, 'da-yai-nu', which means, "it would have been enough".

All sing the hymn: "Now Thank We All Our God"

8. PASSOVER SYMBOLS

Reader No. 7: In Hebrew, Passover is called Pesach. The shank-bone on our Seder plate is the symbol of the Passover lamb that was eaten in the desert in celebration of freedom. In later years Jewish families made a pilgrimage to the Temple in Jerusalem to observe the festival customs. When the Temple was destroyed, the Passover Seder became a home ceremony. How beautiful it is for a family or a congregation to celebrate the Passover in harmony!

Reader No. 8: We eat matzoh all the week of Passover because our fathers ate matzoh when they left Egypt. They were in a great hurry and did not have time to bake ordinary bread. They rolled out their dough on stones and baked it without leaven. The matzoh is a memorial of the poor bread that the children of Israel ate in the desert.

Reader No. 9: We eat bitter herbs to remind us how bitter it was for our ancestors who were slaves in Egypt. The salt water is like the tears that they shed when they were mistreated. The charoseth is a symbol of the bricks that they were forced to make in building the great cities of Egypt.

It is good to remember such bitter things, because we are taught to have sympathy for all who are in trouble. A kind heart is the mark of a good man.

9. HALLEL (Ps 113)

Reader No. 10: It is our duty to thank, praise, and glorify God, who brought our forefathers out of slavery into freedom, from sorrow to joy, from bitterness to gladness, from darkness to light. May we all join in praise of God.

Leader: Praised be the name of the Lord.

All: Praised be His name forever and ever.

Leader: God is high above all nations. His glory is above the heavens.

All: Who is like unto the Lord our God, Who rules all the world?

Leader: Who raises the poor from the dust and lifts the needy out of their troubles.

All: Who brings joy into our life and love into our hearts.

Leader: We praise the Lord with all our soul.

All: We praise the Lord with all our might.

10. SECOND CUP

All (*All elevate the wine cup, recite the wine blessing and drink the second cup*): Praised be Thou, O Lord our God, Ruler of the World, who has created the fruit of the vine. Amen.

11. MATZOH

All (*All break the second matzoh and then recite the following blessings before eating all of the matzoh*): Praised be Thou, O Lord our God, who bring forth bread from the earth.

Praised be Thou, O Lord our God, who made us holy with thy law and commanded us to eat matzoh.

12. BITTER HERBS

Leader reads the following biblical passage: Jn 13, 18-30. Then all dip some bitter herbs in the salt water and eat them.

All (*All recite the following blessing over the bitter herbs mixed with charoseth*): Praised be Thou, O Lord our God, ruler of the universe, who commanded us to eat bitter herbs on Passover.

Leader: Let us recall Christ's words at the Last Supper: "It is one of the twelve, one who is dipping bread in the same dish with me" (Mk 14, 20).

Then all break the third matzoh and make a sandwich of it with the bitter herbs and charoseth and then eat it.

Reader No. 11: (Ex 12, 1-28)

Reader No. 12: (Ex 12, 29-51)

13. EAT SEDER DISHES

The family would then eat the traditional Seder Plate which includes the following: 1. Roasted shankbone of lamb. 2. Hard boiled egg. 3. Bitter herbs cut into small pieces. 4. Charoseth: (a mixture of finely chopped apples, nuts and cinnamon mixed with a little wine). 5. Karas: (either parsley, celery, lettuce, onion or potatoes).

14. BLESSING AFTER THE MEAL

Leader: At this point St. Luke tells us that our Lord took some bread and when he had given thanks he broke it and gave it to the apostles telling them that this was his body which would be given up for them and that they should do the same as a memorial to him. Let us now take the broken particle of matzoh which we had saved for the end of the meal and elevate it and recite together:

We thank Thee, O God, for the food that we have enjoyed and for Thy goodness to all creatures on this earth. We are grateful for this Seder meal. We hope that we shall serve others as we have been served this day. May God give us strength and bless us with peace.

15. THIRD CUP

Leader: Let us here recall that Christ did the same with the cup after supper saying: "This cup which is poured out for you is the new covenant in my blood" (Lk 22, 20). And St. Paul, in his letter to the Corinthians, asks, "The cup of blessing which we bless, is it not a participation in the blood of Christ?" (1 Cor 10, 16).

Let us then recite the following wine blessing, eat the piece of matzoh, and drink the third cup: Praised be thou, O Lord our God, Ruler of the World, who has created the fruit of the vine. Amen.

16. FINAL PRAYER

All: May God bless the whole House of Israel with freedom and keep us safe from danger everywhere. May God bring light to all men that all men may be brothers. May God protect our country as the home of liberty and justice. May He grant peace to us and to all the world.

17. FOURTH CUP

(All sing wine blessing and drink fourth cup. See No. 10)

18. THE GREAT HALLEL

O give thanks to the Lord for he is good,
for his steadfast love endures forever.

O Give thanks to the God of gods,
for his steadfast love endures forever.

O give thanks to the Lord of lords,
for his steadfast love endures forever.

To him who alone does great wonders,
for his steadfast love endures forever.

To him who by understanding made the heavens,
for his steadfast love endures forever.

To him who spread out the earth upon the waters,
for his steadfast love endures forever.

To him who made the great lights,
for his steadfast love endures forever.

The sun to rule over the day,
for his steadfast love endures forever.

The moon and stars to rule over the night,
for his steadfast love endures forever.

To him who smote the first-born of Egypt,
for his steadfast love endures forever.

And brought Israel out from among them,
for his steadfast love endures forever.

With a strong hand and an outstretched arm,
for his steadfast love endures forever.

To him who divided the Red Sea in sunder,
for his steadfast love endures forever.

And made Israel pass through the midst of it,
for his steadfast love endures forever.

But overthrew Pharaoh and his host in the Red Sea,
for his steadfast love endures forever.

To him who led his people through the wilderness,
for his steadfast love endures forever.

To him who smote great kings,

for his steadfast love endures forever.

And slew famous kings,
for his steadfast love endures forever.

Sihon, king of the Amorites,
for his steadfast love endures forever.

And Og, king of Bashan,
for his steadfast love endures forever.

And gave their land as a heritage,
for his steadfast love endures forever.

A heritage to Israel his servant,
for his steadfast love endures forever.

It is he who remembered us in our low estate,
for his steadfast love endures forever.

And rescued us from our foes,
for his steadfast love endures forever.

He who gives food to all flesh,
for his steadfast love endures forever.

O give thanks to the God of heaven,
for his steadfast love endures forever.

19. TOAST TO ELIJAH

Leader: Elijah was a great prophet and teacher long, long ago. Our fathers taught that he comes back to us on Passover Eve at the Seder dinner. Many stories tell how he helps and saves people in trouble. We open the door to Elijah to welcome the thought that all human beings are one family. Each member of the human family has an obligation of brotherhood to all the others. In helping each other, we will be true to Elijah, whose spirit is with us in this Passover season.

CONCLUDING HYMN: "God is Love"

THIRD APPROACH:

A field trip to a synagogue and a home Mass.

OBJECTIVES:
1.   To give the students the actual experience of attending a Passover Service in a synagogue.
2.   To provide them with an opportunity to attend a home Mass to illustrate how the early Christians met in their homes to "break bread."

PROCEDURE:
Contact the rabbi of a nearby synagogue to make arrangements for your class to attend a Passover Service.

Once a day and time has been determined, try to arrange for an evening Mass in one of the student's homes about a week after the visit to the synagogue. If the synagogue service and the Mass follow closely the students will be better able to observe the similarities and differences between the two.

It will probably be more appropriate if you yourself contact the parents to see which ones would be willing to have the Mass at their home. You should also approach the pastor or one of his assistants beforehand to see when they would be available to celebrate the Mass.

Several students will have to volunteer for the following assignments: a) to determine a theme for the Mass and to plan the liturgy, b) to provide refreshments to be served after the home

Mass, c) to assist with the clean-up after the social, d) to write and send "thank you" notes to the rabbi and the parents at whose home the students attended the Mass.

FOURTH APPROACH:

An arts and crafts program entitled, "Giving of Ourselves to Others as Christ Gave to Us."

OBJECTIVES:

1. To make the students more aware of others around them who are in need.

2. To give them an opportunity to express their love and concern for others.

3. To help them realize that their Christian commitment to love and serve others which they express at the Eucharistic meal doesn't end at the Mass but continues throughout the day.

MATERIALS:

Various objects which can be used to make gifts.

PROCEDURE:

First of all, explain to the students that the purpose of this project is to give them an opportunity to show their love and concern for their fellowmen by giving them gifts. They should discuss and decide whether they want to buy the gifts or perhaps make them themselves. They should also discuss to whom they would want to present their gifts. Several examples to consider would be: a home for the aged, an orphanage, a hospital, a day nursery, a younger class in school, a neighbor, etc.

Once they have decided, the class should be divided into groups according to similar preferences. One person in each group should be chosen as a contact person who will be responsible for arranging a day and time convenient for the teacher and the particular institution, grade or home for the group to visit and present their gifts.

Redemption

FIRST APPROACH:

A discussion on the theme: "It is Through Christ that We are Redeemed."

OBJECTIVES:

1. To increase the student's realization of the importance of Christ's redemptive act and how it affects their personal lives.

2. To make them aware of ways in which they can co-operate in Christ's redemptive act by offering up their personal sufferings for the salvation of the world.

3. To inspire them to think of various ways in which they as a class can be helpful to those in need.

MATERIALS:

Discussion sheets, notebooks and pencils.

PROCEDURE:

Distribute the discussion sheets. Have the students read them over carefully and then clarify any questions they may have. They should then break up into small groups to discuss the pivotal questions. After about twenty minutes, the class as a group should have a general discussion period in which the students should summarize the main points brought out in their small group discussions.

Discussion Sheet: "It is Through Christ that We are Redeemed"

First Reader:

We were saved from sin and enabled to enter the kingdom of God, because of the death and resurrection of Christ. St. Paul speaks thus of Christ's obedience:

"If because of one man's trespass, death reigned through that one man, much more will those who receive the abundance of grace and the free gift of righteousness reign in life through the one man Jesus Christ. Then as one man's trespass led to condemnation for all men, so one man's act of righteousness leads to acquittal and life for all men. For as by one man's disobedience many were made sinners, so by one man's obedience many will be made righteous" (Rom 5, 17-19).

PIVOTAL QUESTIONS:

1.   Explain this statement: "Because of one man's trespass, death reigned through that one man."

2.   Did Christ have to die in order to redeem us?

3.   Why is Christ's resurrection a sign that sin is conquered and that all men have regained God's friendship?

Second Reader:

As we read on in the Scriptures we see that all the events of Christ's life give witness to his love and obedience to his Father. We too, like Christ, must experience a certain amount of suffering as well as joy. But it is up to us to bear witness to this fact that we are Christians and our lives are made up of joy, suffering, hunger and rejection.

If we look upon our human weakness as part of us, only then can we begin to accept ourselves. Keep in mind the words of St. Paul concerning our human weaknesses:

"I will all the more gladly boast of my weaknesses, that the power of Christ may rest upon me. For the sake of Christ, then, I am content with weaknesses, insults, hardships, persecutions, and calamities; for when I am weak, then I am strong" (2 Cor 12, 9-10).

PIVOTAL QUESTIONS:

1. Explain this statement: "When I am weak, then I am strong."

2. In what practical ways can we as teenagers help alleviate the sufferings of others?

3. How should we look upon our own personal sufferings?

SECOND APPROACH:

A study of the record "The Life of Christ" (Salesiana Publishers, 148 Main St., New Rochelle, N.Y. 10802) and a dramatization entitled "Christ's Healing Powers."

OBJECTIVES:

1. To familiarize the students with the miracles performed by Christ.

2. To help them understand that Christ came to heal sinners, not to condemn them.

3. To foster a deeper reading of the Scriptures.

4. To enhance teamwork and class participation.

MATERIALS:

The record "The Life of Christ" and a record player.

PROCEDURE:

Explain to the students that the day's lesson will be centered on the miracles Christ performed during his earthly ministry, so that they can come to a better understanding and appreciation of Christ's love and concern for others. These are some of the miracles discussed on the record: a. the curing of the lepers, b. the wedding feast at Cana, c. the curing of the paralytic, d. the bringing back to life of the widow's son, e. the stilling of the tempest, f. the expulsion of demons from two men, g. the bringing back to life of Lazarus, h. the curing of the blind men.

After the playing of the record have the class divide into eight groups. Each group should discuss the various miracles. Then each group can present to the class a dramatization of one of the miracles performed by Christ.

THIRD APPROACH:

A Bible Service on the theme: "Christianity is a Religion of Hope and Joy."

OBJECTIVES:

1. To instill in the students a greater awareness of their commitment to God and their faith.

2. To give them an opportunity to express their commitment in a prayerful way.

3. To stress that they as followers of Christ must bring his message of love and hope to all people.

MATERIALS:

Bible Service sheets, the record "Let the Sunshine In" (*The Fifth Dimension*), a paschal candle and stand, small candles for the whole class.

PROCEDURE:

Distribute the Bible Service sheets and appoint one student to be the leader of the service and three others to be the readers. At the beginning of the service dim the lights and draw the shades. The leader should then enter the darkened room with the lighted paschal candle and place it in the stand in the center of the classroom. Then each student should approach the paschal candle and light his own candle from its flame. When this is done the leader can proceed with the prayer service.

Bible Service: "Christianity is a Religion of Hope and Joy"

Leader:
"I have been crucified with Christ; it is no longer I who live, but Christ who lives in me; and the new life I now live in the flesh I live by faith in the Son of God, who loved me and gave himself for me" (Gal 2, 20).

All:
These words prompt us, dear Lord, to live our faith the best we can as each day comes along.

Leader:
This is because we partake of the Eucharistic meal and are members of Christ's Christian community.

All:
It is because of this witness that we bring Christ's presence to others.

First Reader:
"In the beginning was the Word, and the Word was with God,

and the Word was God. He was in the beginning with God; all things were made through him, and without him was not anything made that was made. In him was life, and the life was the light of men. The light shines in the darkness, and the darkness has not overcome it.

"He was in the world, and the world was made through him, yet the world knew him not. He came to his own home, and his own people received him not. But to all who received him, who believed in his name, he gave power to become children of God; who were born, not of blood nor of the will of the flesh nor of the will of man, but of God" (Jn 1, 1-5, 9-13).

Second Reader:

If we really want to be true followers of Christ, we will have to expect and accept bad times as well as good times, moments of suffering and loneliness as well as moments of happiness and celebration. We have to remember the example of Christ who came into the world to bring love and peace to all men, but was met with hostility and rejection and was even put to death. But we must also remember that Christ rose from the dead and has given us a reason to hope and look forward to eternal life.

Third Reader:

Since we as Christians should be a people full of hope and joy because of our redemption in Christ, we must try to celebrate life with our fellow men. Our life will not end at death—there is a glorious future of eternal life awaiting us. Therefore, we must not only suffer pain with others, but must also share in their joy and happiness. Christianity is truly a religion of hope and joy.

All:

It is high time that we stopped complaining about the dissipation of our world. If we really trusted in God and were truly committed to his purposes, the world might be a great deal better off today. If we dedicate our lives to God, he will be able to work through us to permeate this world's darkness with divine light.

(*This service is then concluded by playing the record* "Let the Sunshine In.")

FOURTH APPROACH:

A discussion based on the short film "The Toymaker."

OBJECTIVES:

    1.   To remind the students that just as Christ reconciled us to his Father, we as Christians have an obligation to help people get along with each other despite differences in color, race or creed.

    2.   To help all the members of the class to accept one another as equals.

    3.   To enhance group morale by participation in class discussions and the making of collages.

MATERIALS:

The film "The Toymaker" (available on rental basis from: Contemporary Films/McGraw Hill, 1714 Stockton St., San Francisco, Ca. 94133 or 828 Custer Ave., Evanston, Ill. 60202 or Princeton Road, Hightstown, N.J. 08520), a movie projector, materials for making collages (cardboard, clippings and photographs from newspapers, magazines, etc.), notebooks and pencils.

PROCEDURE:

    Before showing the film to the class, explain to them that it depicts the idea that we are all different in color, race or creed but we are all the same because of our common Creator—God. Tell them that the toymaker whom they are about to see is a symbol of God, the Creator. He has made two puppets, one with stripes and the other with dots. Tell them to keep in mind the following questions as they view the film.

1.   Why are the puppets always feuding?

2.   What was the main theme or special message of the film?

3.   What did the students personally get out of the movie?

4.   Does it have any application or meaning for their daily lives?

After the class has viewed the movie, have them break up into small groups to discuss the questions so that later on they will be able to contribute their views in the general class discussion. Each group should also make a collage depicting the theme of brotherhood. They can display and explain the collages to the class during the general discussion.

Lent and Penance

FIRST APPROACH:

A discussion on the theme: "The Passion and Death of Our Lord."

OBJECTIVES:

1. To foster a deeper awareness of Christ's complete obedience to his Father and his love for us.

2. To enhance Scripture reading and interpretation.

MATERIALS:

Discussion sheets, Bibles, notebooks and pencils.

PROCEDURE:

Distribute the discussion sheets. The class as a whole should listen attentively to the reading of the Gospel account of the Passion of our Lord. One person should be chosen as the leader. About four or five other readers will be needed to read the account of the Passion of the Lord.

After the reading the class should divide into groups of about four or five for discussion of the pivotal questions. One person in each group should write down the important points discussed so that they can be brought up at the general class discussion.

Discussion Sheet: "The Passion and Death of Our Lord"

Leader:

All during Lent and Holy Week the Church commemorates the Passion of our Lord. The Church vividly points out the depth of Christ's love for his Father and us. Let us now listen attentively to the Gospel account of the Passion of our Lord. (One of the following accounts may be chosen: Mt 26, 14-27, 66; Mk 14, 1-15,47; Lk 22, 14-23,56; Jn 18, 1-19,42).

PIVOTAL QUESTIONS:

1. What do you think you would have done if you had been living during the time of Christ? Would you have accepted or rejected him?

2. In what ways in your own lives do you often act like Judas? Like Peter? Like Pilate?

3. How can you imitate Christ's example of obedience, humility, prayerfulness and forgiveness in your daily lives?

SECOND APPROACH:

Composition writing on the theme: "What Does Lent Mean to Me?"

OBJECTIVES:

1. To stimulate the students to reflect on the interior, personal meaning of Lent in their daily lives.

2. To give them the opportunity to express themselves in creative writing.

MATERIALS:
Notebooks and pencils.

PROCEDURE:
Begin by reminding the students that the Church sets aside the period of Lenten observance as a reminder of Christ's death for our sins and as a time for penance and interior renewal. Then have them write their compositions, keeping in mind the following *pivotal questions*:

1. What are some of the reasons why the Church observes the season of Lent?
2. What meaning does Lent have in this day and age?
3. What meaning does it have for me personally?

The students should then read their compositions to the class. This could then be followed by a discussion of the ideas presented.

THIRD APPROACH:

A dramatic presentation entitled, "Passion Time."

OBJECTIVES:
1. To give the students the opportunity to express their feelings concerning Christ's death and how it affects them personally.
2. To foster group participation through dramatics and discussions.

MATERIALS:
Bibles, notebooks and pencils, materials for making costumes.

PROCEDURE:

Instruct the students that they are to choose some incident from the Gospel account of Christ's passion and death such as the agony in the garden, the betrayal by Judas, Peter's denial of Christ, or the interrogation by Pilate, and are to express their personal feelings by means of role-playing. They should divide into groups based on similar preferences and present their skits to the whole class. This could be followed by a discussion of what feelings motivated them to play their roles the way they did.

This exercise should help the students to summarize and express the ideas they gathered from their previous composition work and discussion sessions.

FOURTH APPROACH:

A communal penitential service.

OBJECTIVES:

1.   To remind the students to prepare for the Lenten penitential season.

2.   To instill in them an awareness of human faults and God's mercy.

3.   To give them an opportunity to gain strength from each other as they participate in this penitential service as a Christian community.

MATERIALS:

Penitential service sheets.

PROCEDURE:

This ceremony should be held in the Church with the pastor or one of his assistants conducting it as the leader. The students should serve as lectors to take care of the readings. It would be good if a general invitation to attend the service were extended to all the parishioners. This would give the students and the parishioners a more profound sense of Christian community. Before the service begins they should be reminded that this service does not replace the need for private confession to a priest in cases of serious sin.

A COMMUNAL PENITENTIAL SERVICE

All:
O give thanks to the Lord, for he is good,
 for his steadfast love endures forever.
O give thanks to the God of gods,
 for his steadfast love endures forever.
O give thanks to the Lord of lords,
 for his steadfast love endures forever (Ps 136, 1-3).

Leader:
 Almighty God, Father of our Savior, Jesus Christ, Creator of heaven and earth and merciful Judge of all mankind, we admit and confess our sins by which we have turned away from you and from each other in our thoughts, words and actions. We are truly sorry for our misdoings and want to repent for our sins. Please be merciful to us because of the obedience of our Brother, Jesus, your Son, who died for our salvation. Forgive us all of our past offenses and inspire us through the power of the Holy Spirit to be more faithful in serving you now and in the future, through Jesus Christ our Lord. Amen.

First Reading: Lk 18, 9-14.

The reading is followed by a period of reflective silence.

Second Reading: Lk 15, 11-32.

HOMILY

The homily is followed by a private examination of conscience. Then all recite the following confession of guilt:

Lord God, to you, but also to all of our fellow brothers and sisters, we confess our guilt in having caused others to suffer because of our self-satisfaction and our selfish disposition. We ask forgiveness from all and we promise that from now on we will have greater respect for others. We humbly ask you, God, to help us to be better, to truly become your image, your likeness. We ask this through Jesus Christ, your Son, our Brother, who has promised to come with the Holy Spirit and dwell in us today and to the end of time. Amen.

Dismissal Rite

Leader:
Let us bless the Lord.

All:
May we continue to grow in the grace and knowledge of our Lord and Savior Jesus Christ. To him be the glory both now and to the day of eternity.

Leader:
Now may the Lord of peace himself give you peace at all times in all ways (2 Th 3, 16).

All:
And may we take hold of it and make it ours.

Leader:
The grace of the Lord Jesus Christ and the love of God and the fellowship of the Holy Spirit be with you all.

All:
Amen.

RECESSIONAL HYMN: "Praise God From Whom All Blessings Flow"

Easter and the Resurrection

FIRST APPROACH:

A Bible study discussion on the theme: "Our Freedom in Christ."

OBJECTIVES:

1. To make the students more conscious of this great Church feast of Easter which is the foundation stone of our faith.

2. To enrich the study of their faith through the use of the Bible.

3. To make them aware of the part they play in the redemptive act.

MATERIALS:

Bibles, Bible study sheets, coat hangers, string, different kinds of scrap material for making mobiles, notebooks and pencils.

PROCEDURE:

Distribute the Bible study discussion sheets. At first discuss them in a general way with the whole class. Then divide the class into small groups for further discussion. Each student should make a mobile on the theme of what freedom means for him. Then each group should report to the class the results of their discussion and display their mobiles.

Discussion Sheet: "Our Freedom in Christ"

OPENING HYMN: "Come Holy Ghost"

Leader:
That Christ's resurrection is the foundation stone of the Christian faith and the greatest proof of Christ's divinity is shown in the following statements from the New Testament:

> "And being found in human form he humbled himself and became obedient unto death, even death on a cross" (Phil 2, 8).

> "I glorified thee on earth, having accomplished the work which thou gavest me to do; and now, Father, glorify thou me in thy own presence with the glory which I had with thee before the world was made" (Jn 17, 4,5).

So that we can better understand the glorification of Christ and all that he has merited for all men through his passion and death which made him a "life-giving spirit" let us read together the following passage from St. Paul: (1 Cor 15, 35-58).

PIVOTAL QUESTIONS:
1.   How can you verify that Christ is the head of the human race?
2.   Give reasons to show that man has benefitted from the actions of Christ?
3.   In what way are we a "free people?"
4.   What effect should this freedom have on the way we act as Christians?
5.   How can Christ's spirit be kept alive in this day and age?
6.   How can I show to the world that I am now a "free

person" because of Christ's death and resurrection?

CONCLUDING HYMN: "Jesus Christ is Risen Today"

SECOND APPROACH:

A group discussion on the theme: "Communication is Sharing Life."

OBJECTIVES:

    1.   To encourage the students to be more open towards one another.

    2.   To make them more aware that all friendships involve risks.

    3.   To help them come to a better understanding of each other through participation in group discussions.

MATERIALS:

Discussion sheets, a record player, the records: "Sounds of Silence" (*Simon and Garfunkel*), "Both Sides Now" (*Judy Collins*) and "Friends" (*Elton John*), notebooks and pencils.

PROCEDURE:

    Distribute the discussion sheets and have the class divide into small groups to discuss the pivotal questions. After a suitable period of time the class as a group should have a general discussion period in which the students should summarize the main points they discussed in their groups.

    As an exercise to summarize their thoughts on communication, sharing and friendship, each student should write a composition about someone he or she admires and give reasons for this admiration. Since these reports may be rather personal, the students shouldn't be obliged to read them to the class but you may ask for volunteers who are willing to share their thoughts.

Discussion Sheet: "Communication is Sharing Life"

Begin by playing the record "Sounds of Silence."

First Reader:

In order to communicate with other people we must have mutual trust, confidence, understanding, faith, love and friendship. But many people in today's world find it difficult and at times impossible to communicate with their fellowmen. There is a lot of talking and gesturing, but it's mostly superficial—there is not much meaningful communication.

Second Reader:

Why is it that although there are so many words to hear and hands to touch they fail to bring people closer together? Why is there so much silence, so much emotional distance between people?

Third Reader:

Maybe it's because it's difficult and sometimes risky for us to try to know, really know, someone else and to have the other person try to really get to know us. It's hard to establish a truly genuine "I-You" relationship. We have to strike a balance between our unique and irreducible identities of "I" and "You" and our desire to share what is common to "us." For to share is to really communicate. And it's a life-long process. But the main thing is to keep on trying to forge ever-deeper levels of communication and friendship not only with our fellowmen but more importantly with God who died for us in order to share with us the gift of everlasting life.

Fourth Reader:

"You yourselves are our letter of recommendation, written on your hearts, to be known and read by all men; and you show that you are a letter from Christ delivered by us, written not with ink but with the Spirit of the living God, not on tablets of stone but on tablets of human hearts" (2 Cor 3, 2-3).

Before the discussion of the pivotal questions, play the following records: "Friends" and "Both Sides Now."

PIVOTAL QUESTIONS:

1.   What are some of the reasons for man's inability to communicate with his fellowmen?

2.   What are some ways in which we can maintain our identities as individuals and still be open to the needs and welfare of others?

3.   How do the above reflections help you to better understand Christ's words: "He who finds his life will lose it, and he who loses his life for my sake will find it" (Mt 10, 39)?

THIRD APPROACH:

Making banners depicting the following themes: "Resurrection," "Freedom," "Reconciliation," "Friendship."

OBJECTIVES:

1.   To give the students an opportunity to think more seriously about their faith and to creatively express their reflections.

2.   To help create a celebrative atmosphere for parish liturgies.

MATERIALS:

Pieces of burlap and old scraps of material suitable for banner making.

PROCEDURE:

Explain to the students that the purpose of this assignment is to have the members of the class creatively portray through banner making some aspect of their faith and to explain what it personally means to them. They could depict such themes as "Resurrection," "Freedom," "Reconciliation," or "Friendship." They could use a biblical quotation or some other motto or maxim. They could decide whether they want to work individually or in groups.

The banners should then be displayed in the church to enhance the celebrative atmosphere of the liturgy.

FOURTH APPROACH:

A Bible Service on the theme: "Christian Reconciliation Within Families."

OBJECTIVES:

1.   To promote a clearer understanding of Christ's redemptive act: Christ's resurrection verifies all that he has come to do for us—to bring us back to God the Father and to reunite us to each other.

2.   To involve both students and parents in a shared prayer experience.

MATERIALS:

Bible Service sheets, invitations to parents to attend the Bible Service, record player, the record "Bridge Over Troubled Water" (*Simon and Garfunkel*).

PROCEDURE:

Speak to the pastor to arrange a convenient evening when he or one of his assistants could conduct a Bible Service for the students and their parents which will be built around the theme of "Christian Reconciliation Within Families." This will be a concrete, practical way of relating Christ's work of reconciliation to the students' everyday lives. It is also a way of getting the parents more involved in their children's spiritual life and will enable all of the families to become better acquainted. If it is feasible, it would be an excellent idea to serve coffee and doughnuts in the parish or school hall after the Bible Service.

The students should form several committees to take care of distributing invitations to the parents, acting as readers during the service, and serving refreshments and cleaning up after the social.

Bible Service: "Christian Reconciliation Within Families"

OPENING HYMN: "Here We Are"

Commentator:

We are all in need of reconciliation. The cutting word or glance that wounds someone we love, the unwillingness to understand the rebuff of efforts to communicate, the stubborn persistence in self-righteousness—this is Everyman. May our hearts be open to receive God's word this evening that we may see ourselves as we really are, that we may examine the poor tattered relationships we have with members of our family, that we may experience a change of heart and be reconciled.

FIRST READING: Mt 5: 20-26 (*after the reading there should be a period of reflective silence during which the record* "Bridge Over Troubled Water" *could be played*).

SECOND READING: 1 Cor 12: 4-11

Congregational Response (*alternate sides*):

L. If I speak in the tongues of men and of angels, but have not love, I am a noisy gong or a clanging cymbal.

R. And if I have prophetic powers, and understand all mysteries and all knowledge, and if I have all faith, so as to remove mountains, but have not love, I am nothing.

L. If I give away all I have, and if I deliver my body to be burned, but have not love, I gain nothing.

R. Love is patient and kind; love is not jealous or boastful; it is not arrogant or rude.

L. Love does not insist on its own way; it is not irritable or resentful; it does not rejoice at wrong, but rejoices in the right.

R. Love bears all things, believes all things, hopes all things, endures all things.

L. Love never ends; as for prophecies, they will pass away; as for tongues, they will cease; as for knowledge, it will pass away.

R. For our knowledge is imperfect and our prophecy is imperfect; but when the perfect comes, the imperfect will pass away (1 Cor 13, 1-10).

THIRD READING: Colossians 3: 12-17

Congregational Response: "They'll Know We Are Christians by Our Love"

HOMILY

Peace Rite—After the homily the peace rite takes place. The priest and all the members of the congregation exchange the greeting of peace. It would be appropriate at this time to sing the hymn: "Christ Is Our Peace!"

FINAL PRAYER: (all say with priest):
  "I do not pray for these only, but also for those who believe in me through their word, that they may all be one; even as thou, Father, art in me, and I in thee, that they also may believe that thou hast sent me. The glory which thou hast given me I have given to them, that they may be one even as we are one, I in them and thou in me, that they may become perfectly one, so that the world may know that thou hast sent me and hast loved them even as thou hast loved me. Father, I desire that they also, whom thou hast given me, may be with me where I am, to behold my glory which thou hast given me in thy love for me before the foundation of the world. O righteous Father, the world has not known thee, but I have known thee; and these know that thou hast sent me. I made known to them thy name, and I will make it known, that the love with which thou hast loved me may be in them, and I in them" (Jn 17: 20-26).

CONCLUDING HYMN: "Whatsoever You Do"

PROCEDURE:

Present the students with the following class assignment: ask them to express in prose or poetry form their thoughts and feelings about Mary, especially how she affects their lives personally. They should entitle their compositions: "What Mary Means to Me."

After the compositions have been read and discussed, several volunteers could neatly type the various essays and poems, illustrate them and compile them into an attractive booklet for the students to keep as a summary of this lesson.

THIRD APPROACH:

Making dioramas or acting out dramatizations on the theme: "Important Events in Mary's Life."

OBJECTIVES:

1. To enhance a deeper understanding of Mary and her role in Christ's redemptive mission.

2. To encourage the use of the Bible as a reference work.

3. To enable the students to express their ideas in a creative project.

MATERIALS:

Bibles, shoe boxes and old scraps of paper and other materials suitable for making dioramas, materials for making costumes.

PROCEDURE:

Explain to the students that they are to look for incidents in the Gospel in which Mary is mentioned, for example, the Annunciation scene, the marriage feast at Cana, and to recreate the scene by means of a diorama or dramatization.

When the dioramas are finished and the dramatizations have

been planned, they should display and explain their dioramas or act out their dramatizations for the class. If it is feasible, they could make costumes to enhance the presentations.

FOURTH APPROACH:

A Mass for the students and their parents, with the theme: "Mary, Our Model of Worship," followed by a social hour.

OBJECTIVES:

1. To give the students and their parents the opportunity to express their love for Mary by attending Mass together.
2. To enrich their knowledge of Mary's role in the Gospel.
3. To foster an appreciation of Mary's titles and honors.
4. To help reinforce a good class spirit by having all the students plan and participate in the liturgy.
5. To encourage teamwork by having them make banners for the liturgy.

MATERIALS:

Bibles, pieces of burlap and other materials suitable for making banners, invitations to be sent to parents, refreshments for the social hour.

PROCEDURE:

If possible, the Mass should be arranged for some evening during the week so that a maximum number of parents will be able to attend. You can discuss this with the pastor and decide upon a convenient day and time.

The students should form committees to take care of inviting the parents, planning the liturgy, providing refreshments for the social hour and cleaning up afterwards. Perhaps another group could make some banners depicting some of Mary's titles, such as Queen of Heaven or Mother of God. This would enhance the celebrative atmosphere during the Mass.

My students have also successfully hosted several social hours after several of the morning Masses. They invite everyone attending the Mass to share coffee and doughnuts with them. This is another effective way of fostering class spirit and encouraging them to become more involved in serving the larger Christian community in which they live.

The following outline could be used for the student-parent Mass in honor of Mary:

Mass Theme: "Mary, Our Model of Worship"

Entrance Hymn: "Sing of Mary"

First Reading: Zacharia 9: 9-10 (*followed by a period of silent reflection*).

Leader: Alleluia, Alleluia, Alleluia

All: Alleluia, Alleluia, Alleluia

Leader:
Sing aloud, O daughter of Zion;
    shout, O Israel!
Rejoice and exult with all your heart,
    O daughter of Jerusalem!
The Lord has taken away the
    judgments against you,
    he has cast out your enemies.
The King of Israel, the Lord,
    is in your midst;
    you shall fear evil no more.

On that day it shall be said to Jerusalem:
  Do not fear, O Zion.

All: Alleluia, Alleluia, Alleluia

SECOND READING (Gospel): Luke 1:39-56

OFFERTORY HYMN: "Into Your Hands"

COMMUNION HYMN: "Where Charity and Love Prevail"

RECESSIONAL HYMN: "Hail, Holy Queen"

Christ's Second Coming

FIRST APPROACH:

A discussion on the theme: "Christ Will Come Again."

OBJECTIVES:
1. To enrich the students' study and appreciation of Scripture.
2. To promote serious thinking on the students' part about their faith in eternity and their obligations to build up God's kingdom here on earth.

MATERIALS:
Discussion sheets, Bibles, notebooks and pencils.

PROCEDURE:
Distribute the discussion sheets and divide the class into small groups to discuss the various readings and pivotal questions. After a sufficient period of time have the secretaries in each group report the main points of discussion. Then the whole class should enter into a general discussion of the main topics.

Discussion Sheet: "Christ Will Come Again"

FIRST READING: I Thessalonians 4:13-18; 5:1-24.

PIVOTAL QUESTIONS:

1. What will be some of the signs preceeding Christ's second coming?

2. How does St. Paul instruct the people to prepare for Christ?

3. How can we as twentieth-century Christians prepare for the Parousia?

SECOND READING: 2 Thessalonians 1:3-12; 1-17.

PIVOTAL QUESTIONS:

1. How does St. Paul describe God's judgment at the end of the world?

2. How should we as followers of Christ prepare for the last judgment?

3. What reasons do we have for hoping that we will be saved at the last judgment?

THIRD READING:

In announcing the kingdom of heaven, Christ promised us eternal salvation. But we must try to have a clear concept of the world to come: the kingdom of God is not built on any human claims or achievements. It does not encourage the worldly ambitions of powerful and privileged people, and is absolutely opposed to any idolization of culture and politics. It is a promise independent of external and visible success and is not concerned with human prowess. The kingdom of God lies in eternity, beyond the short span of our earthly life: it means eternal life with God.

Nevertheless, the kingdom of God has truly appeared in our own lives, visibly and tangibly, with the coming of the incarnate Word of God. It has assumed a human form in the humility, love and kindness of Christ who bears the burdens of all men and directs everything to God's glory. The soul which abandons itself entirely to Christ, the Anointed One, is already united with all the redeemed. It is as if all creation had been waiting to enjoy the first fruits of redemption in Christ's disciples, and now to some extent actually shares in these. Already, here on earth, the family of the redeemed can do the will of God, "as in heaven," if they love him. The expectation of salvation "in the world to come" is based wholly and exclusively on what God has already revealed. When we believe in God's work of salvation we already see the outlines of the new heaven and the new earth.

Our hope is not in liberation from the prison of the flesh but in the body's resurrection; not joy of individual souls only, but a joyful union in the glorification of our love for the Holy Trinity, in communion with the saints, and in universal brotherly charity. By glorifying God's work of redemption and enjoying the hope which urges us onwards, our present obligations and possibilities of salvation are not diminished but are enriched with the greatest possible profundity and significance. It will not be through any diminishment of our hope for eternal life that we will liberate our energies for service to our fellowmen and to the world of today and give us a sense of responsibility for future generations. But we must have a true understanding of eschatological hope. Since Christian hope is based on the fully visible union of Christ with all men and all creatures and aims at universal brotherhood, we find a practical expression of our gratitude and of our expectation in our present obligation to work for increased human solidarity and brotherliness, justice and righteousness. (From *The Church on the Move* by Bernard Haring, C.Ss.R., Alba House, N.Y., 1970).

PIVOTAL QUESTIONS:

1. What are some of the characteristics of the world to come promised by Christ?

2. How has the kingdom of God already become a part of our earthly lives?

3. What are some of the identifying marks of true Christian hope?

SECOND APPROACH:

Performing volunteer works of service in the parish community.

OBJECTIVES:
1. To encourage the students to be more active witnesses to their faith.
2. To foster group team work.
3. To give the students the opportunity to execute their ideas and develop a sense of responsibility.

PROCEDURE:
Discuss with the students the various ways they can perform works of service in their parish community. You could write on the blackboard all the suggestions, such as:
1. Babysitting during Sunday Masses to free more parents to attend Mass.
2. Serving coffee and doughnuts after Mass on Sunday to foster community spirit among the parishioners.
3. Staying with a shut-in so that another member of the family can attend Mass.
4. Visiting old age homes, hospitals, orphanages, etc.
The students can then decide what groups to join. Each group should choose a leader. A weekly or bi-monthly report should be given to the class as to how the groups are progressing in their activities. This service-oriented approach should awaken in the students a spirit of responsibility and a greater realization that their talents can be a great asset in the parish.

THIRD APPROACH:

Making murals depicting the theme: "Outstanding Events in the Life of Christ."

OBJECTIVES:

    1. To make the students more aware of Christ's redemptive love for His followers.

    2. To encourage greater use of the Bible as a reference work.

    3. To foster group participation and enhance good peer relationships.

MATERIALS:

Blackboard or shelf paper, various water color paints, Bibles.

PROCEDURE:

    Divide the class into groups of three or four. Each group should choose one incident in the life of Christ, such as the miracle at the wedding feast at Cana, the feeding of the multitudes, the healing of the sick, etc. They should then make murals illustrating the Christ-event they have chosen to portray. Each group should then display and explain its mural to the rest of the class.

FOURTH APPROACH:

Making mobiles depicting the theme: "The Second Coming of Christ—How I Can Witness to It."

OBJECTIVES:

    1. To reinforce the meaning of Christ's Second Coming.

2. To foster a more personal devotion to Christ.
3. To enhance group participation.

MATERIALS:
Coat hangers, old scraps of cloth, newspapers, cardboard, magazines and other materials for making mobiles.

PROCEDURE:
The class should be divided into groups of three or four. Explain to the class that each group's mobile should depict how Christ's Second Coming affects the students personally, and what effect it has on their faith-life. Each group should then display and explain the mobiles to the other members of the class.

SPECIAL PROGRAMS

I—BOOK STUDIES

OBJECTIVES:
1. To correlate literature with a religion lesson.
2. To make religion lessons a more informative and enjoyable experience.
3. To foster group discussion and participation.

MATERIALS:
Books, notebooks and pencils.

PROCEDURE:
Employing book studies in the religious education program is one of the most effective ways of presenting to teenagers some of the major problems that confront contemporary society, such as racial prejudice, drug abuse, violence, etc. You should assign books to be read to coincide with a particular lesson. For example, if the theme of the lesson is peer-group acceptance, *The Outsiders* by S. E. Hinton (Viking Press, N.Y., 1967) or *The Cross and the Switchblade* by David Wilkerson (Pyramid, N.Y., 1970) would make excellent discussion starters. A list of themes and pertinent books will be found in the Resource Materials Section at the end of this book.

The students should decide which books they would like to read and then small discussion groups can be formed according to similar preferences. Each group should choose a discussion leader. You should present each group with appropriate evaluation questions and discussion starters and decide how much time should be allotted for reading and discussing the books. One person in each group should write down the main points discussed so that they can be presented to the class for general discussion.

II—RECORD STUDIES

THEME A: *Loneliness*

OBJECTIVES:

1.   To help the students realize that they can help others by extending a helping hand to someone in need.

2.   To enrich a religion lesson by using modern day songs and by showing the relevancy of their message to the theme being studied.

3.   To foster class discussion and the sharing of insights.

MATERIALS:

A record player, the records: "Eleanor Rigby" (*The Beatles*), "Within You Without You" (*The Beatles*), "Alfie" (*Dionne Warwick*) and "Georgy Girl" (*The Seekers*); notebooks and pencils.

PROCEDURE:

Distribute the record study sheets which can be based on the outline presented below. You can determine how much time should be spent for the discussion of each song and how many songs to discuss, depending on your particular classroom situation.

After the general discussion it would be good to give the students some time for silent reflection on the main points discussed so that they can write an essay on some of the ways they can overcome some of the problems associated with their own personal loneliness and the loneliness experienced by their friends.

Outline of Record Study on "Loneliness"

INTRODUCTION:

Jesus Christ often preached the message of love of God and love of neighbor. St. Paul wrote one of the most beautiful descriptions of true love in I Cor 13: 1-13. In our modern music, love is described in so many ways. In order to grow love has to be nurtured. People have to deal with one another as humans, not objects. We have to learn to live out Christ's commandment to love one another by sharing and caring, not just talking about it. We have to learn to accept others and their limitations. We must bridge the gap of loneliness which separates so many people today. The following songs will help us to understand more clearly how we can give love to others in a society so empty of it.

I. *"Eleanor Rigby"*
You find lonely people looking for someone to talk to but afraid to take the step. They retreat into themselves and face whatever is left of life alone.

PIVOTAL QUESTIONS:

1. Why are people like Eleanor Rigby and Fr. McKenzie lonely?
2. Are they facing life?
3. Does society have a responsibility to help people like Eleanor Rigby? What can we do personally to help such people?

II. *"Within You Without You"*
This song depicts the theme that we are all one if only we do

away with our masks of phoniness and be ourselves. Only then can we be more self-giving rather than being selfish.

PIVOTAL QUESTIONS:

1.   What is the song trying to tell us about people who try to hide themselves behind walls of illusion?

2.   What kind of love can we share with each other?

3.   Can someone force you to love or can you force someone to love you?

III. *"Alfie"*

This song depicts the life of a playboy in urban society. The questions posed by the song affect our own lives and the attitudes we form towards ourselves and those with whom we live.

PIVOTAL QUESTIONS:

1.   Can you explain in your own words what it means to live just for the moment? Do many people espouse this philosophy today?

2.   Why does Alfie call those who love "fools"?

3.   Can one exist without love?

IV. *"Georgy Girl"*

Georgy Girl is a lonely person but doesn't want anyone to notice it. She puts on a great act but deep down she knows that she is not "for real" and is afraid to admit it. Many of us are afraid to show our true emotions and therefore are afraid to be ourselves. This is dangerous for we not only hurt ourselves but those who know us too.

PIVOTAL QUESTIONS:

1.   What would your reactions be if you were to meet up with a "Georgy Girl"?

2.   Are you a "for-real" person?

3. Do you think that the advertising world has a lot to do with producing "Georgy Girls"?

CONCLUDING REMARKS:

The love of Christ has proven that all men should cease to live for themselves and should live for him who died and was buried for their sake. We have to remember that when one is united with Christ a shedding of the old self takes place and the putting on of the new has begun in us.

THEME B: *Communication*

OBJECTIVES:

1. To make the students more aware of the many types and levels of communication.

2. To help them realize that it's up to them to begin breaking down the barriers to communication which they face.

3. To encourage class discussion and the sharing of insights.

MATERIALS:

A record player, the records: "Sounds of Silence" (*Simon and Garfunkel*), "People" (*Barbra Streisand*), "Born Free" (*Roger Williams*), "Getting Better" (*The Beatles*), "I'm Looking Through You" (*The Beatles*), notebooks and pencils.

PROCEDURE:

Distribute the record study sheets which can be based on the outline presented below. You can determine how much time should be spent for the discussion of each song and how many songs to discuss, depending on your particular classroom situation.

After the general discussion it would be good to give the

students some time for silent reflection on the main points discussed so that they can write an essay expressing their ideas concerning interpersonal communication and practical ways in which they can begin to break down barriers of communication between themselves and God and other people.

Outline of Record Study on "Communication"

INTRODUCTION:

Conversations can be made on different levels and yet this depends a lot on the people involved. You can have a poet expressing himself in a poem, a writer by means of his book, a saint by his aesthetic ways. A conversation can be silent or verbose depending on the nature of it. It can be between people or between objects and people or between people and God.

I. "Sounds of Silence"

PIVOTAL QUESTIONS:

1. Why is darkness called "my old friend"?
2. What kind of vision is the writer talking about?
3. What do you mean when you say a person is listening but not hearing?

II. "People"

PIVOTAL QUESTIONS:

1. Can you explain why some people tend to act like children more than children do themselves?
2. Do you have to need people in order to survive today?
3. Is it hard to be a good friend to someone?

III. *"Born Free"*

PIVOTAL QUESTIONS:

1. Are we really free when we can't communicate this freedom?

2. How would you explain to someone the idea that all men are born free?

3. If you were given your freedom what would you do with it?

IV. *"Getting Better"*

PIVOTAL QUESTIONS:

1. Do you think the singer likes to be bogged down with rules?

2. What was the turning point that made him feel he had a hopeful life ahead of him?

3. Do you agree that things are getting better?

V. *"I'm Looking Through You"*

PIVOTAL QUESTIONS:

1. How many of you have experienced talking to someone and not being heard?

2. Can you see through a person? Explain.

3. How can you break down the barriers to communication?

CONCLUDING READINGS:

"You yourselves are our letter of recommendation, written on your hearts, to be known and read by all men; and you show that you are a letter from Christ delivered by us, written not with ink but with the Spirit of the living God, not on tablets of stone but on tablets of human hearts" (2 Cor 3: 2-3).

We have ears to hear but no one is listening.

We have words to speak but no one is talking.
We have hands to touch but no one is touching.
Why, Lord, is there so much silence? Why does
     all this distance exist?
All I ask is to pass beyond and beneath
     the "other self" of us all.
To communicate by sharing, acting and not merely talking,
     touching hearts and souls and being close to you.

O God, I feel so alone,
It's so hard at times—
For no one seems to care
but you, O Lord.

I want so much to have a friend
And yet it's so hard to give of myself.
Help me to believe in you and in others,
and to feel that you'll always be my friend.

Keep me from being made a fool of.
Keep me from being bitter toward those
who use me.
Help me to see only the beauty that lies
within the person I meet.
I want to believe that you are my friend.
I want to believe that others are too.
Thank you for letting me just "be".
Thank you for becoming "We".

III.—CREATIVE WRITING PROJECTS

OBJECTIVES:

     1.   To give the students an opportunity to increase in self-awareness and self-esteem.

2. To enhance their values and attitudes toward life and their role in the Church and society.

3. To enable them to creatively express themselves and reveal their personalities to others.

4. To help the teacher come to a better knowledge of her class.

MATERIALS:

Notebooks and pencils.

PROCEDURE:

Listed below are five creative writing projects which you can adapt and use according to your particular classroom situation, the amount of time available, etc. Using some creative ingenuity you will be able to devise some projects of your own which will enable the students to organize and express in writing their inner feelings and attitudes and help you to become acquainted with the different personalities of your students. If time permits, they could read their essays to the rest of the class and a general discussion of some of the more outstanding insights could follow.

Five Creative Writing Projects

1) Have the students write compositions on the following themes: a) What do you value most in life? b) What is your philosophy of life? c) If you had the freedom to do as you pleased, what would you do?

2) Direct the students to reflect for a few minutes on some particular talent that God has given them and then have them write a brief essay on what the talent means to them and how they should use it to help others.

3) Play some thought-provoking records as "Bridge Over

Troubled Water" (*Simon and Garfunkel*) or "Morning Has Broken" (*Cat Stevens*) as background music to help create a reflective mood. The room should be dimly lit with four-color wheels in motion to produce something of a psychedelic effect. After a suitable period of reflection, have the students write down their personal reflections on the lyrics of the song.

4) Ask the students to complete the statement: Love is.... with the first five ideas that come to their minds. Then you can discuss the statements with the class. It's amazing to see the ideas they come up with about love and other subjects.

5) Have the students rewrite in their own words one of the Psalms or have them take some quotations from the Bible which interest them and explain the particular meaning these sayings hold for them.

IV—PEOPLE'S DAY

OBJECTIVES:

1. To encourage the students to get involved with less fortunate students from the inner city.

2. To give them an opportunity to form new friendships by sharing and respecting other people's opinions and values.

3. To foster class esprit de corps through group cooperation in hosting this day of friendship and brotherhood in a spirit of unselfish giving of love and service to others.

MATERIALS:

Invitations, refreshments, materials for making banners.

PROCEDURE:

The students themselves should be in charge of handling the activities of People's Day with the teacher overseeing the whole project. Two students should be selected to serve as chairman and co-chairman. It will be their responsibility to organize various committees to take care of sending out the invitations, planning the liturgy, making identification cards, making welcoming banners, providing refreshments, planning entertainment, and cleaning up after the day is over. Every student should be involved in some activity.

The class invited from the inner city should be at the same grade level as your students so that there will be a common basis for meaningful discussion and sharing of ideas on topics such as love, friendship, community spirit and brotherhood.

The day's activities should commence with the celebration of Mass which the students themselves should plan. Then the discussion should follow. The students will easily begin to develop friendships with each other as they openly discuss common problems, goals and values and learn to listen to and respect one another's ideas. A sing-a-long or some other form of entertainment could follow the discussion period. After this, refreshments could be served and the program could conclude with the presentation of the welcoming banners to the visiting class as meaningful souvenirs of this wonderful day of sharing, loving and learning.

V.—PSYCHEDELIC ENCOUNTERS

Theme A: *Looking to the Future*

OBJECTIVES:

1. To develop the students' self-esteem and impress upon them the fact that each one of them has a unique and valuable role to play in today's world as a Christian.

2. To make the religion lesson "come alive" for them.

3. To combine a learning situation with a prayerful experience.

MATERIALS:

Strobe lights or color wheels, multi-colored lights, black light, overhead projector, a white screen or sheet, two clear pyrex plates, food coloring, oil, record player, records: "I've Gotta Be Me" (*Sammy Davis Jr.*), "The Long and Winding Road" (*The Beatles*), "I Wanna Be Free" (*The Monkees*), "Born Free" (*Roger Williams*), "Climb Every Mountain" (*Mary Martin*); refreshments, notebooks and pencils.

PROCEDURE:

This encounter using psychedelic lighting effects can be held in the school hall or classroom. Two students should be selected to act as chairman and co-chairman. They should appoint various committees to take care of seating arrangements, refreshments, decorations, psychedelic lighting and visual effects, music coordination and clean-up. Several readers will have to be selected to take care of the ten short readings, and two students should be chosen to give brief talks on the following themes: 1. "Looking Forward to the Future" and 2. "What Do We Have to Offer?" Finally, several students should be chosen to lead the discussions of the pivotal questions after each song.

The following procedure for making the best use of psychedelic lighting and visual effects could be used. The strobe lights or color wheels and the black light will help to create a mood of reflection and meditation in a semi-darkened room. The students could also hang some pictures or photographs around the room.

While the various records are being played you can project onto the white screen or sheet or wall a psychedelic effect produced by using two clear pyrex pie plates over an overhead projector. The bottom plate contains oil and food coloring. You then place the empty pie plate on the other plate and move it in such a way that different designs appear on the screen or sheet or wall. While this is going on the hall or room should be darkened to make the lighting effective in setting the appropriate mood while the record is playing.

The following outline can be used for this psychedelic encounter:

THEME: "Looking to the Future"

First Reader:
O God, we are gathered here today because we really want to get to know you better and try to find out what the future means to us.

Second Reader:
Please make us open ourselves to your Son as we meet him in this encounter.

Third Reader:
It is not always possible to know when someone is doing something constructively or where his work may lead him.

MEDITATION SONG: "I've Gotta Be Me"

PIVOTAL QUESTIONS:
1. How many of you have dreams of what your future holds for you?
2. Are you daring enough to try to reach this goal?
3. Would you be willing to accept help in reaching your goal in life?

Fourth Reader:
Lord, how can I be me in a world that is only concerned with material things and not human persons?

Fifth Reader:
Do I stand a chance of making use of my talents?

Sixth Reader:
Every generation hungers for life and love. It's up to us to try to make it a reality here and now.

SHORT TALK: "Looking Forward to the Future" (*given by one of the students*).

MEDITATION SONG: "Climb Every Mountain"

PIVOTAL QUESTIONS:
    1.   When you have a problem do you seek help?
    2.   Do you have the courage of your convictions to face your problems in order to follow your dream?
    3.   Are you willing to share this dream with someone?

SHORT TALK: "What Do We Have to Offer?" (*given by one of the students*).

MEDITATION SONG: "The Long and Winding Road"

PIVOTAL QUESTIONS:
    1.   Even though the struggle is hard, are you willing to go on?
    2.   People can be very selfish. How will you deal with their selfishness?
    3.   Do you agree with this statement: "Life is a gamble; therefore I too ought to take part in the game"?

Seventh Reader:
Lord, I realize that the talents you have given me are to be used to help make this world a better place in which to live. Whether

I will be a doctor, a nurse, a teacher, a scientist, or a religious, I will have to do my best to make a go of it, and thereby fulfill your will.

Eighth Reader:
A true Christian always preserves his sense of wonder.

Ninth Reader:
The meaning of life depends, then, not only on what one possesses but, more importantly, on the way one uses what he has.

MEDITATION SONGS: "I Wanna Be Free" and "Born Free"

PIVOTAL QUESTIONS:
    1.   How many of you want to be free in order to grow?
    2.   How many of you want to be free to do away with responsibility? Is this true freedom?
    3.   Are you really free if you love someone?

Tenth Reader:
Yes, Lord, we are born free to follow our hearts and therefore life's worth living. Help us always to seek that true freedom which enables us to follow you and love you with all our heart.

THEME B: *A Time for Understanding and Love*

OBJECTIVES:
    1.   To give the students and their parents the opportunity to get together for an evening of reflection during which they can share their views and ideas in open dialogue.
    2.   To foster a better understanding between the students and parents as they attempt to mutually bridge the "generation gap."

3. To help them realize that perhaps the "generation gap" is not so much that, but rather a "communication gap", and with more listening, love and understanding, this gap could close.

MATERIALS:

Letters of invitation to parents, strobe lights or color wheels, black light, overhead projector, a white screen or sheet, two pyrex plates, food coloring, oil, record player, records: "Within You Without You" (*The Beatles*), "Let's Work Together" (*The Youngbloods*), "She's Leaving Home" (*The Beatles*), "Isn't It a Pity?" (*The Beatles*); refreshments, notebooks and pencils.

PROCEDURE:

This evening of reflection, listening and dialogue between the students and their parents should be held in the school hall or gym to insure comfortable seating arrangements and to make the best possible use of the psychedelic lighting effects.

Letters of invitation should be sent to the parents, outlining the purpose of the encounter and the activities planned. The parents should be asked to indicate whether or not they will attend, the number attending, as well as the evening and time which would be most convenient for them to attend.

Various committees will have to be appointed to take care of the seating arrangements, refreshments, decorations, psychedelic lighting and visual effects, music coordination and clean-up. Seven students should be selected as lectors to take care of the short readings. About a month prior to the encounter, those students who have volunteered to lead the discussion groups should remain after school about two nights a week for instructions in group discussion techniques.

On the evening of the encounter the parents and students should break up into small discussion groups with the leader conducting the discussions of the pivotal questions after each record has been listened to. Then a general discussion could follow with spokesmen from each group presenting a summary of the main points discussed. The program could then conclude with the serving of refreshments.

The following outline could be used for this student-parent night of reflection and encounter:

THEME: "A Time for Understanding and Love"

Opening remarks of introduction and welcome given by teacher.

First Reader:
The age of understanding begins to grow with moments of insight.

Second Reader:
It comes and goes, but sometimes bits of understanding and compassion stay.

Third Reader:
At times we see for just a moment how others think and feel and then we know how much alike we are.

Fourth Reader:
We also see how we share ourselves in different ways.

MEDITATION SONG: "Within You Without You"

PIVOTAL QUESTIONS:
1. How can we keep the love we've found within our families?
2. How can we share our family love with others?
3. Has love died out in our society?

Fifth Reader:
Why do we put up barriers to communication and love?

Sixth Reader:
Could it be that we are afraid to take the risk of loving?

Seventh Reader:
It is in the family that life, faith, and love are enhanced. The family is the most effective sign we have of the relationship between life, faith, and love.

MEDITATION SONG: "Isn't It a Pity?"

PIVOTAL QUESTIONS:
    1.   Why does it seem that it's easier to hurt and hate other people rather than love them?
    2.   What are some of the ways in which we take other people for granted?
    3.   What is some of the beauty around us that we often forget to see? Maybe the joy of being in love, the tears of sadness wiped away by a consoling hand, people working hard to support families because they love them?

MEDITATION SONG: "Let's Work Together"

PIVOTAL QUESTIONS:
    1.   Does life have to be all "peaches and cream" in order to be a good life?
    2.   Is your life always going to consist in making people happy?
    3.   What is the unity that we are striving for?

MEDITATION SONG: "She's Leaving Home"

PIVOTAL QUESTIONS:

    1.   Why did the girl leave a note?

    2.   Did she think that leaving home would solve the problem?

    3.   Why was there so little communication between the girl and her parents?

A general discussion period follows the discussion in the individual groups.

The program concludes with the serving of refreshments.

RESOURCE MATERIALS

Selected Reading List

Ashbrook, James B.
   Be-Come Community, Judson Press, Valley Forge, Pa.,
   1971.

Audinet, Jacques
   Forming the Faith of Adolescents, Herder and Herder, New
   York, 1968.

Babin, Pierre
   Audiovisuals, Pflaum, Dayton, Ohio, 1970.

Boros, Ladislaus, S.J.
   God Is With Us, Herder and Herder, New York, 1967.

Brandt, Leslie F.
   God Is Here—Let's Celebrate, Concordia Publishing House,
   St. Louis, Mo., 1970.

Brusselmans, Christiane
   Religion for Little Children, A Parents' Guide, Our Sunday
   Visitor, Huntington, Ind., 1970.

Carroll, James P.
   Feed My Lambs, Pflaum, Dayton, Ohio, 1964.

Castagnola, Lawrence, S.J.
   Confessions of a Catechist, Alba House, New York, 1970.

Coudreau, Francois, P.S.S.
   Basic Catechetical Perspectives, Paulist, New York, 1969.

Daly, Lowrie J. and Daly, Sr. M. Virgene
   Meditations from Advent to Lent, Sheed and Ward, New York, 1966.

Daughters of St. Paul
   The Catechism of Modern Man, Daughters of St. Paul, Boston, Mass., 1970.

Devine, George
   Transformation in Christ, Alba House, New York, 1972.

Diekmann, Godfrey, O.S.B.
   Come, Let Us Worship, Helicon Press, Baltimore, Md., 1961.

Durrwell, Francis X., C.Ss.R.
   In the Redeeming Christ, Towards a Theology of Spirituality, Sheed and Ward, New York, 1963.
   The Resurrection, Sheed and Ward, New York, 1960.

Gales, Louis A. and Hartman, Charles, *The Old Testament*, Guild Press, New York, 1963.

Geaney, Dennis J., O.S.A.
   You Shall Be Witnesses, Fides, Notre Dame, Ind., 1963.

Goldman, Ronald
   Readiness for Religion, Seabury, New York, 1968.

Religious Thinking from Childhood to Adolescence,
Seabury, New York, 1968.

Havighurst, Robert J.
The Education Mission of the Church, Westminster,
Philadelphia, Pa., 1965.

Heyer, Robert, S.J. (ed.)
Discovery in Prayer, Paulist, New York, 1969.
Discovery in Song, Paulist, New York, 1968.

Hogan, William F.
Christ's Redemptive Sacrifice, Prentice-Hall,
New Jersey, 1963.

Hubbard, Celia (ed.)
*Let's See: The Use and Misuse of Visual Arts in Religious
Education,* Paulist, New York, 1966.

Jeep, Elizabeth
Classroom Creativity, Herder and Herder, New York, 1970.

Lee, James M., and Rooney, Patrick (eds.)
Toward a Future for Religious Education, Pflaum, Dayton,
Ohio, 1970.

McBride, Alfred
Catechetics: A Theology of Proclamation,
Bruce, Milwaukee, Wisc., 1966.
The Human Dimension of Catechetics, Bruce, Milwaukee,
Wisc., 1969.

McHugh, P.J.
Living the Christian Life, Bruce, Milwaukee, Wisc., 1967.

McIntyre, Marie (ed.)
Aids for Religion Teachers: Some Procedures and Techniques, Our Sunday Visitor, Huntington, Ind.,'1968.
Aids for Religious Teachers: Teaching Teens, Our Sunday Visitor, Huntington, Ind., 1968.

McKenzie, Leon
Christian Education in the 70s, Alba House, New York, 1971.
Process Catechetics, Paulist, New York, 1970.

Montessori, Maria
The Discovery of the Child, Fides, Notre Dame, Ind., 1957.

Mourier, Trophine
The Creation, Hawthorn, New York, 1962.

Mueller, Alois (ed.)
Catechetics for the Future, Herder and Herder, New York, 1970.

Mussen, Paul H.
The Psychological Development of the Child, Prentice-Hall, New Jersey, 1963.

Newland, Mary Reed
Homemade Christians, Pflaum, Dayton, Ohio, 1964.

Nicolas, Marie Joseph
What is the Eucharist?, Hawthorn, New York, 1962.

O'Doherty, Eamonn F.
The Religious Formation of the Elementary School Child,

Alba House, New York, 1973.
The Religious Formation of the Adolescent, Alba House,
New York, 1973.

O'Neill, Robert, and Donovan, Michael
Children, Church & God, Corpus, Washington, D.C., 1970.

Orem, R.C. (ed.)
A Montessori Handbook, Putnam, New York, 1966.

Padovano, Anthony T.
American Culture and the Quest for Christ, Sheed and
Ward, New York, 1970.
Belief in Human Life, Paulist, New York, 1969.
Dawn Without Darkness, Paulist, New York, 1970.
The Estranged God: Modern Man's Search for Belief,
Sheed and Ward, New York, 1966.
Free to be Faithful, Paulist, New York, 1972.
Who is Christ?, Ave Maria Press, Notre Dame, Ind., 1970.

Pierini, Franco, S.S.P.
Catechism of Vatican II, Alba House, New York, 1967.

Pitlyk, Jean, C.S.J.
Media in High School Religion: A Journal, Pflaum,
Dayton, Ohio, 1970.

Posset, Franz
American Catechetics: Personal and Secular, St. Mary's
College Press, Winona, Minn., 1969.

Pottebaum, Gerard A., and Winkel, Joyce
1,029 Private Prayers for Worldly Christians,
Pflaum, Dayton, Ohio, 1969.

Powell, John, S.J.
Why Am I Afraid to Love?, Argus Communications, Chicago, Ill. 1970.
Why Am I Afraid to Tell You Who I Am?, Argus Communications, Chicago, Ill., 1970.

Quoist, Michel
Christ is Alive, Doubleday, New York, 1971.
Prayers, Sheed and Ward, New York, 1963.
The Meaning of Success, Fides, Notre Dame, Ind., 1965.

Rahner, Karl, S.J.
Grace in Freedom, Herder and Herder, New York, 1969.
On Prayer, Paulist, New York, 1969.
Watch and Pray With Me, Herder and Herder, New York, 1966.

Ranwez, Pierre
The Dawn of the Christian Life, Paulist, New York, 1970.

Ratzinger, Joseph
Being Christian, Franciscan Herald Press, Chicago, Ill., 1971.
Faith and the Future, Franciscan Herald Press, Chicago, Ill., 1971.
Introduction to Christianity, Herder and Herder, New York, 1970.
Open Circle: The Meaning of Christian Brotherhood, Sheed and Ward, New York, 1966.

Reichert, Richard
Self-Awareness Through Group Dynamics, Pflaum, Dayton, Ohio, 1972.
Xpand: Experiencing Christianity, Ave Maria Press, Notre

Dame, Ind., 1970.

Renckens, Henry
Israel's Concept of the Beginning, Herder and Herder, New York, 1964.

Rivers, Clarence
Celebration, Herder and Herder, New York, 1969.
Reflections, Herder and Herder, New York, 1970.

Roensch, Roger C.
The Mass and Sacraments For Teenagers, Paulist Press, New York, 1965.

Rosenbaum, Jean
Becoming Yourself: The Teen Years, St. Anthony Messenger Press, Cincinnati, Ohio, 1971.

Ryan, Mary Perkins
Helping Adolescents Grow Up in Christ, Paulist, New York, 1970.
Key to the Psalms, Liturgical Press, Collegeville, Minn., 1970.
Psalms Seventy: A New Approach to Old Prayers, Pflaum, Dayton, Ohio, 1969.

Schoonenberg, Piet
The Christ, Herder and Herder, New York, 1971.

Sheed, Frank J.
What Difference Does Christ Make?, Sheed and Ward, New York, 1970.

Short, Robert L.

The Gospel According to Peanuts, Bantam Books, New York, 1970.

Skillin, Joseph
Bread and Wine in the Now Generation, Pflaum, Dayton, Ohio, 1969.

Stillmock, Martin, C.Ss.R.
Teens Talk of Many Things, Alba House, New York, 1972.

Sullivan, Ed
Walter Fish, Alba House Communications, Canfield, Ohio, 1969.

Todd, John M.
The Laity: The People of God, Paulist Press, New York, 1967.

Toffler, Alvin
Future Shock, Random House, New York, 1970.

van der Poel, C.J.
Man, The Living Expression of God, Paulist, New York, 1971.
The Search for Human Values, Paulist, New York, 1971.

van Zeller, Hubert
Approach to Calvary, Sheed and Ward, New York, 1961.
Approach to Penance, Sheed and Ward, New York, 1958.
Approach to Prayer, Sheed and Ward, New York, 1959.
Ideas for Prayer, Templegate, Springfield, Ill., 1966.
More Ideas for Prayer, Templegate, Springfield, Ill., 1967.
The Psalms in Other Words, Templegate, Springfield, Ill., 1964.

Vawter, Bruce, C.M.
A Path Through Genesis, Sheed and Ward, New York, 1956.

Vergote, Antoine
The Religious Man, Pflaum, Dayton, Ohio, 1969.

von Balthasar, Hans Urs
Prayer, Paulist, New York, 1970.
Way of the Cross, Herder and Herder, New York, 1970.
Who Is a Christian?, Paulist, New York, 1971.

Wilhelm, Anthony J., C.S.P.
Christ Among Us: A Modern Presentation of the Catholic Faith, Paulist, New York, 1971.

Willett, Franciscus, C.S.C.
Our Christian Beginnings, Holy Cross Press, N.Y., 1966.

Yperman, Joseph
Teaching the Eucharist, Paulist, New York, 1970.

Books for Teaching with Audio-Visual Resources

Abels, Paul and Barbara
Discover and Create, Friendship Press, New York, 1970.

Babin, Pierre
The Audio-Visual Man, Pflaum, Dayton, Ohio, 1970.

Bigler, Lewis
Rock Theology: Interpreting the Music of Youth Culture,

Benziger Bros., New York, 1970.

Bluem, A. William (ed.)
Religious Television Programs, Hastings House, New York, 1968.

Cooper, John and Skrade, Carl (eds.)
Celluloid and Symbols, Fortress Press, Philadelphia, Pa., 1970.

Cushing, Jane, I.B.V.M.
One Hundred One Films for Character Growth, Fides, Notre Dame, Ind., 1969.

Dalglish, William A., Beaubien, Roger E., and Laude, Walter R. (eds.)
Media for Christian Formation, Pflaum, Dayton, Ohio, 1967.
Media Two for Christian Formation, Pflaum, Dayton, Ohio, 1970.

Dispensa, Joseph
Reruns: A Study Guide for Selected Films on TV, Benziger Bros., New York, 1970.

Feyen, Sharon and Wigal, Donald
Screen Experience: An Approach to Film, Pflaum, Dayton, Ohio, 1970.

Fischer, Edward
Film as Insight, Fides, Notre Dame, Ind., 1971.
Screen Arts: A Guide to Film and Television Appreciation, Sheed and Ward, New York, 1969.

Giardino, Thomas, F.S.M., and Kuhns, William
Behind the Camera, Pflaum, Dayton, Ohio, 1970.

Hurley, Neil P.
Theology Through Film, Harper and Row, New York, 1970.

Kuhns, William
Short Films in Religious Education, Pflaum, Dayton, Ohio, 1970.
The Electronic Gospel, Religion and Media, Herder and Herder, New York, 1969.
Themes: Short Films for Discussion, Pflaum, Dayton, Ohio, 1970.
Why We Watch Them: Interpreting TV Shows, Benziger Bros., New York, 1970.

McCaffrey, Patrick J.
Films for Religious Education, Vol. I, Fides, Notre Dame, Ind., 1967.
Films for Religious Education, Vol. II, Fides, Notre Dame, Ind., 1968.

Mohs, Mayo A.
Other Worlds, Other Gods: Adventures in Religious Science Fiction, Doubleday, New York, 1971.

Ostrach, Herbert F.
Youth in Contemporary Society, Espousal Retreat Center, 554 Lexington St., Waltham, Mass. 02154, 1970.

Parrington, Ruth
An Educator's Guide to the Use of Film, Argus Communi-

cations, Chicago, Ill., 1970.

Reile, Louis
Films in Focus, Abbey Press, St. Meinrad, Ind., 1970.

Savary, Louis M., S.J.
The Kingdom of Downtown: Finding Teenagers in Their Music, Paulist, New York, 1968.

Schillaci, Anthony
Movies and Morals, Fides, Notre Dame, Ind., 1968.

Schrank, Jeffrey
Media in Value Education, Argus Communications, Chicago, Ill., 1970.

Sohn, David A.
Film: The Creative Eye, Pflaum, Dayton, Ohio, 1970.

Sullivan, Bede, O.S.B.
Movies: Universal Language, Fides, Notre Dame, Ind. 1967.

Wyman, Richard
Mediaware: Selection, Operation and Maintenance, Brown, Dubuque, Iowa, 1969.

Periodicals

The Living Light
Noll Plaza

Huntington, Indiana 46750

The Catechist
38 West Fifth Street
Dayton, Ohio 45402

Religion Teacher's Journal
P. O. Box 180
West Mystic, Connecticut 06388

Today's Catholic Teacher
38 W. Fifth St.
Dayton, Ohio 45402

Religious Education
545 W. 111th Street
New York, New York 10025

Mass Media Ministries
2116 N. Charles Street
Baltimore, Maryland 21218

Educational Media
Seccombe House
443 Mount Pleasant Road
Toronto 7, Ontario

Books for Special Themes

BROTHERHOOD

Dooley, Thomas A.

Doctor Tom Dooley, My Story, New American Library, New York, 1970.

Myers, Elisabeth P.
Angel of Appalachia: Martha Berry, Julian Messner (Division of Simon and Schuster), New York, 1968.

Sechrist, Elizabeth H. and Woolsey, Janette
It's Time for Brotherhood, Macrae Smith Co., Philadelphia, Pa., 1962.

COURAGE AND DETERMINATION

Archibald, Joseph
Right Field Rookie, Macrae Smith Co., Philadelphia, Pa., 1967.
The Scrambler, Macrae Smith Co., Philadelphia, Pa., 1967.

Ashe, Geoffrey
Gandhi, Stein and Day, New York, 1969.

Beim, Lorraine
Triumph Clear, Harcourt, Bruce, Jovanovich, Inc., New York.

Dooley, Thomas A.
Doctor Tom Dooley, My Story, New American Library, New York, 1970.

Frick, C. H.
Comeback Guy, Harcourt, Brace, Jovanovich, Inc., New York.

Jackson, Caary P., and Jackson, O. B.
Freshman Forward, McGraw-Hill, New York.

Jacobs, Helen H.
Famous American Women Athletes, Dodd, Mead and Co.
New York, 1964.

Kayira, Legson
I Will Try, Doubleday, New York, 1965.

Keller, Helen
The Story of My Life, Airmont, New York.

Killilea, Marie
Karen, Dell, New York.
With Love From Karen, Dell, New York.

Simon, Charlie M.
Dag Hammarskjold, E.P. Dutton and Co., New York,
1967.

Washington, Booker T.
Up From Slavery, Airmont, New York.

JUDAISM

Frank, Anne
Anne Frank: Diary of a Young Girl, Doubleday, New York,
1967.

Potok, Chaim
The Chosen, Simon and Schuster, New York, 1967.

The Promise, Fawcett World Library Crest Book, New York.

Wiesel, Elie
The Jews of Silence, New American Library, New York, 1967.

PEER GROUP ACCEPTANCE

Harris, John D.
The Junkie Priest, Pocket Books, Inc., New York.

Hinton, S.E.
The Outsiders, Viking Press, New York, 1967.

Jackson, Caary P., and Jackson, O.B.
Freshman Forward, McGraw-Hill, New York.

Melody, Roland
The Narco Priest, World Publishing Co., Cleveland, Ohio.

Offit, Sidney
Cadet Quarterback, St. Martin's Press, New York, 1961.

Wilkerson, David
The Cross and the Switchblade, Pyramid Publications, New York, 1970.
Hey Preach, You're Comin' Through, Pyramid Publications, New York, 1971.

THE RACIAL QUESTION

Gault, William C.
Drag Strip, Berkley Publishing Corp., New York.

Washington, Booker T.
Up From Slavery, Airmont, New York.

RELIGIONS OF THE WORLD

Ashe, Geoffrey
Gandhi, Stein and Day, New York, 1969.

Elgin, Kathleen
The Episcopalians, David McKay Co., New York, 1970.
The Mormons: The Church of Jesus Christ of Latter-Day Saints, David McKay Co., New York, 1969.
The Quakers: The Religious Society of Friends, David McKay, Co., New York, 1968.
The Unitarians, David McKay Co., New York, 1971.

Fitch, Florence M.
Their Search for God: Ways of Worship in the Orient, Lothrop, Lee and Shephard Co., New York, 1944.

Kjelgaard, Jim A.
The Coming of the Mormons, Random House, New York, 1953.

Parrinder, Geoffrey
The Faith of Mankind: A Guide to the World's Living Religions, Thomas Y. Crowell Co., New York, 1965.

Savage, Katherine
The Story of World Religions, Henry Z. Walck, Inc., New York, 1967.

Whalen, William J.
Minority Religions in America, Alba House, Staten Island,

New York, 1972.

UNDERSTANDING OF ONE'S SELF

Fedder, Ruth
  A Girl Grows Up, McGraw-Hill, New York, 1967.

McKown, Harry C.
  A Boy Grows Up, McGraw-Hill, New York.

Noshpitz, Joseph D.
  Understanding Ourselves: The Challenge of the Human Mind, Coward, McCann and Geoghegan, Inc., New York.

Quoist, Michel
  With Love, Ann Marie, Newman Press, New York, 1968.

VALUES

Archibald, Joseph
  Pro Coach, Macrae Smith Co., Philadelphia, Pa., 1969.
  Quarterback and Son, Macrae Smith Co., Philadelphia, Pa., 1964.
  Right Field Rookie, Macrae Smith Co., Philadelphia, Pa., 1967.
  Southpaw Speed, Macrae Smith Co., Philadelphia, Pa., 1966.

Companies From Which to Request Catalogues

Abbey Press
St. Meinrad, Ind. 47577

Alba House
2187 Victory Blvd.
Staten Island, N.Y. 10314

Alba House Communications
Canfield, Ohio 44406

Alba House Media
7050 Pinehurst
Dearborn, Mich. 48126

American Friends Service
160 N. 15th St.
Philadelphia, Pa.

Argus Communications
3505 N. Ashland Ave.
Chicago, Ill. 60657

Association Films
600 Madison Ave.
New York, N.Y. 10022

Audio Film Center
2138 E. 75th St.
Chicago, Ill. 60649

Audio Film Classics
406 Clements St.

San Francisco, Calif.

Audio-Visual Extension Ser.
University of Minnesota
2037 University Ave., S.E.
Minneapolis, Minn. 55455

Augsburg Publishing House
Films Department
426 5th St.
Minneapolis, Minn.

Avant Garde Records
250 W. 57th St.
New York, N.Y. 10019

Ave Maria Press
Notre Dame, Ind. 46556

Benziger Brothers, Inc.
866 Third Ave.
New York, N.Y. 10022

BFC TV Films
475 Riverside Drive
New York, N.Y. 10027

Brandon Films, Inc.
221 W. 57th St.
New York, N.Y. 10019

Bureau of Audio-Visual
Services

The University of Arizona
Tucson, Arizona 85721

Carousel Films
1501 Broadway
New York, N.Y. 10036

Catechetical Guild
262 E. 4th St.
St. Paul, Minn. 55101

Cathedral Films
2921 W. Alameda Ave.
Burbank, Calif. 91505

CCM Films, Inc.
866 Third Ave.
New York, N.Y. 10022

Center for Film Study
21 West Superior St.
Chicago, Ill. 60010

Claretian Publications
221 West Madison St.
Chicago, Ill. 60606

Contemporary / McGraw-Hill
Princeton Rd
Hightstown, N.J. 08520

Continental 16
241 E. 34th St.
New York, N.Y. 10016

Creative Film Library
1455 Valerio St.
Van Nuys, Calif. 91405

Creative Resources
Box 1790
Waco, Texas 76703

Curriculum Innovations, Inc.
5454 South Shore Drive
Chicago, Ill. 60615

Daughters of St. Paul
50 St. Paul Ave.
Jamaica Plain
Boston, Mass. 02130

Divine Word Publications
Techny, Ill. 60082

Don Bosco Filmstrips
Box T
New Rochelle, N.Y. 10802

Eastman Kodak Co.
Rochester, N.Y. 14650

Educational Film Library Assn.
250 W. 57th St.
New York, N.Y. 10019

Educators Guide to Free Films
Educators Progress Service
Randolph, Wisconsin 53936

Embassy Pictures
Time-Life Bldg.
New York, N.Y. 10020

Espousal Retreat Center
554 Lexington St.
Waltham, Mass. 02154

Extension Lay Volunteers
1307 S. Wabash Ave.
Chicago, Ill. 60605

Extension Media Center
University of California
2223 Fulton St.
Berkeley, Calif. 94720

Family Enrichment Bureau
1615 Ludington St.
Escanaba, Mich. 49829

Family Films and Filmstrips
5823 Santa Monica Blvd.
Hollywood, Calif. 90020

Family Theater
7201 Sunset Blvd.
Hollywood, Calif. 90020

F.E.L. Publications
1307 South Wabash Ave.
Chicago, Ill. 60605

F.E.L. Publications

1543 West Olympic Blvd.
Los Angeles, Calif. 90015

Fides Publishing Co.
Notre Dame, Ind. 46556

Films Distribution Division
University of Southern Calif.
University Park
Los Angeles, Calif. 90007

Films Incorporated
5625 Hollywood Blvd.
Los Angeles, Calif.

Films Incorporated
1150 Wilmette Ave.
Wilmette, Ill. 60091

Franciscan Herald Press
1434 W. 51 St.
Chicago, Ill. 60609

Friendship Press
475 Riverside Drive
New York, N.Y. 10027

The Grail
Loveland, Ohio 45140

Grove Press Film Library
80 University Place
New York, N.Y. 10003

Guidance Associates
23 Washington Ave.
Pleasantville, N.Y. 10570

Herder and Herder, Inc.
232 Madison Ave.
New York, N.Y. 10016

HI-TIME Visual Aids
Box 7337
Milwaukee, Wisc. 53213

Holt, Rinehart and Winston
383 Madison Ave.
New York, N.Y. 10017

Ideal Audio Visual
4431 W. North Ave.
Milwaukee, Wisc. 53208

Ideal Pictures
1010 Church St.
Evanston, Ill. 60201

Indiana University
Audio-Visual Center
Bloomington, Ind. 47401

Insight Films
Paulist Productions
17575 Pacific Coast Highway
Pacific Palisades, Calif. 90272

Instructional Media Center

Michigan State University
East Lansing, Mich. 48823

Janus Films
745 5th Ave.
New York, N.Y. 10019

John P. Daleiden Co.
1530 N. Sedgwick St.
Chicago, Ill. 60610

Kairos Films
6412 Indian Hills Road
Minneapolis, Minn. 55435

Koinonia Records
617 Custer St.
Evanston, Ill. 60202

Learning Corp. of America
711 5th Avenue
New York, N.Y. 10022

Life Filmstrips
Time-Life Building
Rockefeller Center
New York, N.Y. 10020

Life-Long Learning Through
Films
University of Calif. at L.A.
Westwood, Calif.

Liguorian Press

Liguori, Mo. 63057

Liturgical Arts Guild
314-S.W. Washington St.
Portland, Oregon 97204

Liturgical Press
St. John's Abbey
Collegeville, Minn. 56321

Mass Media Ministries
2116 N. Charles St.
Baltimore, Md. 21218

McDougal, Littell and Co.
P.O. Box 1667
Evanston, Ill. 60204

McGraw-Hill Film Dept.
Manchester Road
Manchester, Mo. 63011

Modern Talking Picture Ser.
1212 Avenue of Americas
New York, N.Y. 10036

Museum of Modern Art Films
11 W. 53rd St.
New York, N.Y. 10019

National Catholic Office for
Motion Pictures
453 Madison Ave.
New York, N.Y. 10022

National Center for Film
Study
1307 S. Wabash Ave.
Chicago, Ill. 60605

National Council of Catholic
Men
405 Lexington Ave.
New York, N.Y. 10027

National Council of Churches
Guide
475 Riverside Drive
New York, N.Y. 10027

National Film Board
of Canada
680 Fifth Ave.
New York, N.Y. 10019

National Film Board
of Canada
P.O. Box 6100
Montreal 3, Quebec, Canada

The National Newman
Apostolate
1312 Mass. Ave., N.W.
Washington, D.C. 20005

NCCM Film Center
405 Lexington Ave.
New York, N.Y. 10017

New York University
Film Library
26 Washington Place
New York, N.Y. 10003

Novalis
1 Stewart St.
Ottawa 2, Canada

Our Sunday Visitor Press
Noll Plaza
Huntington, Ind. 46750

Pathe Contemporary Films
39 W. 55th St.
New York, N.Y. 10019

Paulist Press
400 Sette Drive
Paramus, N.J. 07652

Paulist Productions
17575 Pacific Coast Highway
Pacific Palisades, Calif. 90272

Geo. A. Pflaum, Publisher
38 West Fifth St.
Dayton, Ohio 45402

QED Productions
A Division of Cathedral Films
P.O. Box 1608
Burbank, Calif.

Regina Press
7 Midland Ave.
Hicksville, N.Y. 11801

The Reigner Recording Lib.
Audio-Visual Center
Union Theological Seminary
Richmond, Va. 23227

Roa's Films
1629 N. Astor St.
Milwaukee, Wisc. 53202

Sheed and Ward
64 University Place
New York, N.Y. 10003

Silver Burdett Company
Park Ave. & Columbia Rd.
Morristown, N. J. 07960

St. Anthony Messenger Press
1615 Republic St.
Cincinnati, Ohio 45210

St. Clement's Film Assn.
423 W. 46th St.
New York, N.Y. 10036

St. Francis Productions
1229 S. Santee St.
Los Angeles, Calif. 90015

St. Mary's College Press

Winona, Minn. 55987

St. Paul Films
7050 Pinehurst
Dearborn, Mich. 48126

St. Rochus Audio-Visual
Library
314 Eights Avenue
Johnstown, Pa. 15906

Standard Film Service
4418 Pearl Road
Cleveland, Ohio 44109

Sterling Educational Films
241 E. 34th St.
New York, N.Y. 10016

Sterling Movies
43 W. 61st St.
New York, N.Y. 10023

Swank Motion Pictures
621 N. Skinker St.
St. Louis, Mo. 63130

Thomas S. Klise Co.
P.O. Box 3418
Peoria, Ill. 61614

Trans-World Films
323 S. Michigan Ave.
Chicago, Ill. 60604

Twenty-Third Publications
P.O. Box 180
Ft. Wayne, Ind. 46801

Twyman Films, Inc.
329 Salem Ave.
Dayton, Ohio 45401

Union Theological Seminary
Audio-Visual Dept.
3041 Broadway
New York, N.Y. 10027

United Artists
729 7th Ave.
New York, N.Y. 10019

United World Films
221 Park Ave. South
New York, N.Y. 10003

Univ. of Southern California
School of Performing Arts
Film Distribution Section
University Park
Los Angeles, Calif. 90007

Visual Aids Service
University of Illinois
Champaign, Ill. 61822

Walt Disney Films
250 Buena Vista St.
Burbank, Calif. 91503

Additional
Books
from
Alba House

BE-ATTITUDES By Claude J. Farley

 The author, 1967 winner of the NCEA "Impact Teacher" award, relates how he has succeeded in bringing the message of Christ to teenagers. Utilizing the yearning of young people to love the unloved, he has developed a scripturally-based program to apply the Christian message in concrete situations of poverty and loneliness. This approach prompts the students to examine life and form sound religious value judgments in terms of "Be-attitudes"—their basic attitudes toward being and toward being Christians. The approach is unique, exciting . . . and it works.

$1.35, ppr.

CATECHISM OF VATICAN II
Ed. by F. Pierini, S.S.P.

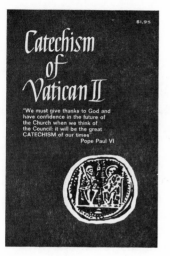

This is a handbook of the Council's thinking reduced to a simple well-organized question and answer format.
$1.95, ppr.

PRESENTING CHRIST
By Sr. Maria de la Cruz Aymes

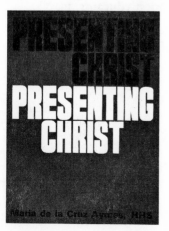

The co-author of ON OUR WAY series crystallizes best CCD thinking on critical catechetical problems. $1.75, ppr.

RELIGIOUS FORMATION OF THE ELEMENTARY SCHOOL CHILD
By E. F. O'Doherty, Ph.D.

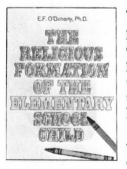

This book, by the noted priest-psychologist Prof. O'Doherty, discusses from a psychological aspect the religious formation of the child during the critical elementary school years. The author describes how children act at each stage of development and then discusses the reasons for these acts. He discusses such topics as sin, use of reason, and juvenile delinquency along with many others. His conclusions are practical and tempered with the concern expected of a priest-educator in discussing the formation of future Christians.

$3.95

ELECTIVES FOR REVITALIZING HIGH SCHOOL RELIGION
By Sr. M. Michael, I.H.M.

This noted educator and author presents a Christ-centered and Scripture-orientated high school religion program utilizing ELECTIVES and MINI-ELECTIVES and based on the method of laboratory instruction, team teaching, and student involvement.

Of great value is the well-researched and up-to-date resource materials section which is included. It lists many of the books, pamphlets, films, records and other audio-visual materials which teachers can use in planning their elective programs as well as informative suggestions on how they could be best implemented.

"Many good ideas and much information about programs and materials." SPIRITUAL BOOK NEWS

$4.95, ppr.